Praise for THE KIDS' GUIDE TO WORKING OUT CONFLICTS

"Naomi Drew knows that conflict avoidance is not the answer to conflict resolution. She provides essential skills for teens to listen respectfully, discuss sincerely, decide empathically, and proceed with empowerment."
—**Maurice J. Elias, Ph.D.,** coauthor of *Raising Emotionally Intelligent Teenagers*

"A complete and practical toolkit to help navigate a sometimes hostile world. Although it never minimizes the difficulties of dealing with angry or mean people, it makes staying cool and dignified seem both desirable and doable."
—**Meg Cox,** author of *The Book of New Family Traditions*

"Naomi Drew's colorful and attractive *The Kids' Guide to Working Out Conflicts* builds on the experience of many of today's middle schoolers in turning ugly situations into opportunities for positive relationships."
—**Elise Boulding,** Professor Emerita of Sociology, Dartmouth College, former Secretary General of the International Peace Research Association, and author of *Cultures of Peace*

"This book leaves readers with everyday strategies to work out conflicts, and, as a result, become happier in their relationships with their family and friends. Naomi Drew offers her readers the hope that every day is an opportunity to change."
—**Christopher J. Campisano, Ed.D.,** New Jersey Department of Education

"I heartily recommend *The Kids' Guide to Working Out Conflicts* to any parent or child—or world leader for that matter."
—**Greg Martin,** coauthor of *The Buddha In Your Mirror*

"Naomi Drew has written a wonderful book for kids on how to deal effectively with anger, conflict, stress, and bullying in order to lead a more satisfying, peaceful, resilient life. Her ideas are presented in an easy-to-read style and her suggestions are very practical and achievable. Not only will kids find this book an invaluable resource, but so too will their parents and other caregivers."
—**Dr. Robert Brooks,** faculty Harvard Medical School, author of *The Self-Esteem Teacher*, and coauthor of *Raising Resilient Children*

"*The Kids' Guide to Working Out Conflicts* is a must read for every adult who interacts with children—parents, teachers, administrators, group leaders—and should be on every home library shelf. Parents and children can use it together to confront everyday issues such as friendship, responsibility, feelings and bullying. This book is truly an incredible resource and is exactly what we have been waiting for."
—**Maureen Pfeffer,** member of the New Jersey PTA Board of Directors

"This book should be read by every child, parent, teacher—anyone who guides and nurtures children. It beautifully points the way to a kinder, more cooperative culture. Naomi Drew wisely shows kids how to tap into their inner power and wisdom to ease their conflicts, talk out their differences, stay calm, find common ground, and create great peace. She is a master teacher and a pathfinder in our culture."
—**Susan Skog,** author of *Radical Acts of Love* and *Embracing Our Essence*

A LEADER'S GUIDE TO

THE KIDS' GUIDE TO

Working Out
CONFLICTS
How to Keep Cool, Stay Safe, and Get Along

NAOMI DREW, M.A.

free spirit
PUBLISHING®

Helping kids
help themselves™
since 1983

ISBN 1-57542-154-2

At the time of this book's publication, all facts and figures cited are the most current available; all telephone numbers, addresses, and Web site URLs are accurate and active; all publications, organizations, Web sites, and other resources exist as described in this book; and all have been verified as of July 2004. The author and Free Spirit Publishing make no warranty or guarantee concerning the information and materials given out by organizations or content found at Web sites, and we are not responsible for any changes that occur after this book's publication. If you find an error or believe that a resource listed here is not as described, please contact Free Spirit Publishing. Parents, teachers, and other adults: We strongly urge you to monitor children's use of the Internet.

The "Win/Win Guidelines," first cited on page 40, are adapted from *Learning the Skills of Peacemaking* (revised edition) by Naomi Drew (Torrance, CA: Jalmar Press, 1995). Used with permission.

Edited by Al Desetta
Cover design by Marieka Heinlen
Index by Ina Gravitz

10 9 8 7 6 5 4 3 2 1
Printed in the United States of America

Free Spirit Publishing Inc.
217 Fifth Avenue North, Suite 200
Minneapolis, MN 55401-1299
(612) 338-2068
help4kids@freespirit.com
www.freespirit.com

Dedication

This book is dedicated to teachers and all others who work with kids. You're shaping the world through the lives you touch.

Acknowledgments

I would like to thank the following people:

- My editor, Al Desetta, for his wisdom and keen eye.

- Editorial director at Free Spirit, Margie Lisovskis, for her top-level editorial skills.

- Publisher, Judy Galbraith, for her deep commitment to kids.

- All the wonderful people at Free Spirit who helped make this book possible.

- All the teachers, counselors, administrators, and kids whose words and thoughts play a big part in this guide.

- The STOP group at the Hudson Bend Middle School in Austin, Texas, for their honesty, insight, and commitment to eradicating cruel behavior among middle schoolers

- Mandy Lehrman's 2003–4 class at the Paul Robeson School, in Trenton, New Jersey, for their insights about what's on the minds of kids.

- My husband, Mel Baum, for his continual love and support.

Contents

Preface

Why Teach Conflict Resolution? ix

Introduction

Tailoring This Book to Your Setting 1

Coordinating with the Curriculum 1

How the Sessions Are Organized 2

Setting Ground Rules 2

Using the Sessions 3

Getting Started 5

Evaluating Students' Learning 5

The Sessions

An Open Mind

Session 1: Why Learn
to Resolve Conflicts? 11

Session 2: What Starts a Conflict?
What Makes It Grow? 14

Session 3: Willingness Is the Key 17

Session 4: Basement or Balcony—
Making the Choice 19

Deciding to Become a Conflict Solver

Session 5: Using "Stop, Breathe, Chill"
to Solve Conflicts 22

Session 6: The Dignity Stance:
Taking a Peaceful Stand 26

Session 7: Learning
from Conflict Solvers 31

Listening

Session 8: Listening
to Help Solve Conflicts 33

Session 9: How to Spark a Turnaround . . . 37

Using Win/Win Guidelines

Session 10: Using I-Messages 40

Session 11: The Win/Win Guidelines:
Taking Responsibility
to Help Resolve Conflicts 44

Session 12: The Win/Win Guidelines:
Brainstorming Solutions
and Affirming the Other Person 47

Session 13: Applying
the Win/Win Guidelines
to Real-Life Conflicts 50

Managing Anger

Session 14: Understanding
and Gaining Control of Your Anger 53

Session 15: Becoming Zinger-Proof 56

Session 16: Using Visualization
to Stay Cool 58

Managing Stress

Session 17: Coping with Stress 60

Session 18: Peaceful Place Visualization . . . 63

Session 19: The Secret of 5/25 66

Being Smart About Bullying

Session 20: Dealing with Teasing 68

Session 21: Standing Up
for Someone Who Is Being Bullied 70

Session 22: Responding to Being Bullied . . . 74

Building Personal Power

Session 23: Spreading the Word
About Working Out Conflicts 76

Session 24: The Power of Forgiveness 78

Session 25: Using a Day-by-Day Plan 81

Supplemental Materials

What I've Learned About Working Out
Conflicts (Steps 1–8) 93

What I've Learned About Working Out
Conflicts (Final Summary Test) 101

What I've Learned About Working Out
Conflicts (Answer Key) 103

Resources 106

Survey 109

Index 111

About the Author 115

List of Reproducible Pages

Note to Family Adults (school setting) 7

Note to Family Adults
(youth group setting) 8

Observing Conflict 13

My Conflict Triggers 16

Basement or Balcony:
Which Did You Choose? 21

When I Have a Conflict 24

Conflict Log 25

Conflict Solver Interview 29

Dignity Stance 30

Check Out Your Listening 35

What Good Listeners Do 36

The Win/Win Guidelines
and Rules for Using
the Win/Win Guidelines 43

Taking Responsibility 46

Using Brain Power to Find Solutions 49

Conflict Resolution Observation Sheet 52

Managing Anger 55

When I'm Under Stress 62

Are You Bullying or Harassing Anyone? . . . 73

Forgiveness Statement 80

Conflict Solver's
Action Plan (Days 1–7) 83–89

What I've Learned
About Working Out Conflicts
Quizzes (Steps 1–8) 93–100

What I've Learned
About Working Out Conflicts
(Final Summary Questions) 101

Working Out Conflicts Survey 109

Preface
Why Teach Conflict Resolution?

"If we wish to have real peace in the world, then we must begin with children."
Ghandi

Teaching the skills of conflict resolution and peacemaking can seem daunting at first. Most of us were never taught in a structured way how to manage anger, resolve conflicts, or express compassion. At the same time, the young people we work with are constantly bombarded with images of aggression and violence in TV shows, movies, and video and computer games.

Today's middle schools face problems caused by emotional and sometimes physical violence. I surveyed over 1,000 middle schoolers nationwide (see the survey on pages 109–110), and 89 percent said their peers are either "somewhat mean" or "very mean" to each other. Eighty percent said they see kids having arguments or fights every day, and 63 percent report having been picked on. According to the National Education Association, 160,000 students skip school daily for fear of being mistreated by their peers. If kids feel unsafe or threatened, they cannot learn.

That's why young people themselves are hungry for solutions. In the same survey, 90 percent said it is important to learn how to peacefully resolve conflicts. As one student said, "If we stopped fighting, our lives would be much better."

While we can't bring violence to a halt, the skills of conflict resolution and violence prevention can make our homes, schools, and communities more peaceful. The young people you are raising and teaching are our greatest hope. Middle schoolers, in particular, are at a unique and exciting stage. They are on the cusp of independence and are searching for ways to define themselves. By teaching and

modeling conflict resolution skills to them now, we can potentially shape their thinking for the rest of their lives. Each time we help them take responsibility for their actions and act with compassion, we are helping them grow into mature, empathic adults. As a former student in my old school, now a teacher herself, once told me: "What I learned about peacemaking when I was younger, I continue to apply in my life."

This leader's guide, used in conjunction with *The Kids' Guide to Working Out Conflicts: How to Keep Cool, Stay Safe, and Get Along*, will give you concrete, proven ways to:

- foster respect and positive communication

- reduce conflict and violence

- teach anger management skills

- build compassion for others

- counter bullying

- fortify young people against the effects of teasing and other hurtful behaviors

- make school a more peaceful place

The power of this book is that it addresses real conflicts in the lives of students. They will be asked to reflect on their actions, to take personal responsibility for solving conflict, and to make more positive choices as a result. The guide is action-oriented, so students will be asked to participate in role plays, conduct interviews, and work cooperatively with their peers. By doing the exercises in this book, they will be guided to question previous assumptions, practice new concepts, and apply what they've learned at school, at home, and in the community.

The leader's guide teaches specific techniques to help students:

- think instead of react

- cool down instead of act out

- listen instead of blame

- walk away from fights

- stand up for themselves assertively, not aggressively

- empathize with others

- help kids who are picked on

The time you invest in teaching these strategies will be regained with less time spent on arguments and conflicts between students. When young people are able to get their feelings and concerns out on the table, they're more open to learning. Nothing shuts down a young person more than an unresolved conflict with a friend or a bullying incident in the schoolyard. The leader's guide gives you an opportunity to get at what students really think about conflict and to help them deal with it in positive ways in their daily lives.

If you are an educator, please share this book with your colleagues and administrators.

If you are a parent or other family adult, please read *The Kids' Guide to Working Out Conflicts* with your child and do the exercises together. Make what you learn from these books a part of your family's life.

If you are a youth group leader, scout leader, or religious education teacher, please use *The Kids' Guide to Working Out Conflicts* and its leader's guide with your group. Talk about how the concepts can be applied to everyday life.

Together, we have the power to put the wheels of peace in motion. Please contact me if you have any questions or experiences to share. You can reach me at:

Free Spirit Publishing Inc.
217 Fifth Avenue North, Suite 200
Minneapolis, MN 55401-1299
email: help4kids@freespirit.com

In peace,

Naomi Drew

Introduction

This leader's guide is designed to be used with *The Kids' Guide to Working Out Conflicts*. The following explains how to use the guide with the student book, how the sessions are organized, and how to get started.

Tailoring This Book to Your Setting

This leader's guide can be used in a wide variety of settings—both in and out of school, with kids in a classroom, a small group, or a youth group setting. You can choose to conduct all 25 sessions, or pick and choose among the sessions for those that best fit your setting and the students' needs.

If you are a classroom teacher and can conduct all 25 sessions, you can do one or two a week and reinforce the concepts between sessions. Consider coordinating with another classroom teacher and collaborating together on group projects.

If you are a school counselor and wish to use this book with small groups that meet weekly, determine which sessions best meet the needs of the group. If you visit existing classes to teach, ask the regular teacher to be a part of the sessions. The results for students will be vastly improved if

classroom teachers understand, apply, and reinforce what is learned in the sessions.

If you are a youth group or community leader and have more flexibility in your schedule, devoting an hour to each session would be ideal. You'll have more time for discussion and activities.

In addition, a one- or two-day retreat can be a powerful way of using the leader's guide to teach conflict resolution. Consider doing three sessions each day—after breakfast, lunch, and dinner. Set aside time for physical activity, and do something light or funny at the end of the day.

Coordinating with the Curriculum

If you are a classroom teacher, every session in this book ties in with either health, social studies, language arts, or character education. You can also relate these sessions to books students are reading, items in the news, or other material they are learning.

In addition, the teaching of conflict resolution and other peacemaking skills is now mandated by federal law, Title IV—21st Century Schools: "Safe and

1

Drug-Free Schools and Communities." Part A, section 4115(b)(2)(E)(viii) calls for the implementation of conflict resolution programs, and section 4115(b)(2)(E)(xiii) calls for:

> "Age-appropriate, developmentally-based violence prevention and education programs . . . that include activities designed to help students develop a sense of individual responsibility and respect for the rights of others, and to resolve conflicts without violence."

The "When I Have a Conflict" checklist in Session 5 (see page 24) is a good pre- and post-sessions assessment of students' progress in dealing with conflicts and a helpful gauge of students' attitudes toward conflict resolution and peacemaking.

How the Sessions Are Organized

This book is organized into 25 sessions that coordinate with the 8 steps of *The Kids' Guide.* The chart on page 6 shows at-a-glance which sessions correspond to each step and the specific page numbers from *The Kids' Guide.*

Every session is about 45 minutes in length and most are structured in the following way:

Students will. What students will learn; the main goals of the session are described here.

Materials. The materials you need to conduct the session. Most handouts are reproducibles. Other materials are easily obtained, such as chart paper and markers.

Preparation. Instructions for preparing for the session are given here.

The session. Detailed instructions are given for conducting the session, organized under the following main categories:

Checking In (usually 10 minutes). Each session begins with a review of a previous assignment, an activity introducing the main theme of the session, or other activities.

Main Activity (usually 25 minutes). The main theme of each session is taught through some combination of large group discussion, paired sharing, role playing, writing, visualizations, or dialogues from *The Kids' Guide.*

Wrap-Up (usually 5–10 minutes). The session is brought to closure through writing, discussion, or other activities.

Looking Ahead. Every session has an assignment for students to complete, such as reading portions of *The Kids' Guide,* interviews, or other activities. All assignments are intended to help students apply what they learn at home and school.

Additional activities. For most of the sessions, I've provided additional activities that relate to the main themes of the session. These activities are designed to help you enrich and deepen the material covered. The additional activities allow you to spend more time on certain concepts or to work on the special needs of the group. Please use and adapt them as you see fit.

Setting Ground Rules

Create an Atmosphere of Safety

Before the first session, start by setting ground rules so you can work together in a nonthreatening atmosphere of support, encouragement, kindness, and nonjudgment. Ask students:

- **What makes you feel safe in a group?** (*For example,* knowing no one will laugh or make faces when they talk.)

- **How do you want group members to treat each other?**

- **What can we do together to create an atmosphere where everyone feels safe, accepted, and respected?**

On chart paper, write the ground rules the students suggest. Add your own ground rules, too. The following are some suggestions:

We Agree to . . .

- listen with an open mind.

- be kind and respectful toward each other.

- not interrupt or make negative comments or faces.

- not judge what people say.

- avoid using specific names when discussing conflicts, saying instead, "this kid" or "someone I know."

- honor confidentiality: keep what we say within the group.

Have students sign the ground rules. You sign them, too, to let students know that you'll be honoring them also. Post the rules in a prominent spot and review them often.

Hold students accountable to the rules and acknowledge the group for honoring them. You can do this verbally, through notes, or even with an occasional call to parents.

Stress Confidentiality

Honoring confidentiality is an important ground rule. However, maintaining confidentiality in a school setting can be almost impossible. Point out to students that in the group they should only talk about things they are comfortable sharing. No one is required to talk or write about highly personal issues.

Students also should not bring other people's personal information into group discussions. Remind students not to use real names when describing a conflict. Coach them to say, "Someone I know," "This kid," "A person in our school," "Someone in my home," or "A relative of mine." This applies to writing assignments as well. Caution students not to share their notebooks with anyone outside of class.

Using the Sessions

Choosing What to Teach

Each session is designed so it builds on the previous one. You will get maximum value from this book if you teach all 25 sessions, but if this isn't feasible or desirable, pick and choose the ones that most fit your needs. Adapt the content to your particular group. If you think something won't work, don't do it.

If your group becomes deeply engaged in a particular discussion or role play and you run out of time, save the remainder of the session for the next time the group meets.

The Kids' Guide contains many activities not covered in the leader's guide. I encourage you to use these exercises and activities as you see fit.

Conducting Role Plays

Role playing is a key learning strategy in this book. Role playing enables students to practice conflict resolution strategies, making it easier to apply them when actual conflicts arise. Only through continued practice will students become confident and comfortable enough to use these strategies effectively in real-life situations.

Using students' experiences with conflict as sources for the role plays is one of the best ways to help them apply the skills in this book. Ask for background on the conflict so the group has a context for what is about to take place. Make sure to get enough detail so the actors are clear on the needs and feelings of each person involved. You may even want to write a few sentences on the board or chart paper describing the nature of the conflict and each person's needs and feelings. Actors can refer to these notes during the role play.

Ask for volunteers to play the parts. If no students volunteer, you can play one of the parts yourself. If the actual conflict resulted in a fight, have them pantomime the movements.

Here are basic ground rules for role plays:

- Students are not required to participate in role plays, or, if they do participate, to reveal personal information they are not comfortable sharing.

- No physical contact or use of swear words is allowed.

- Actors should never use real names.

- If the actors get offtrack or start to act silly, stop the role play and remind them of its purpose and the ground rules.

In many of the sessions, the players act out the conflict as it actually occurred, and then replay it using conflict resolution skills that are featured in the session.

During the role play, the rest of the students need to pay close attention to the actors' behavior, body language, and tone of voice, and be ready to give feedback at the end. Talk about this ahead of time. You might want to encourage them to take notes as they observe. Feedback will provide vital insight into what made the conflict escalate, become stalemated, or get resolved.

Managing Discussions

If possible, have students sit in a circle. This helps them make eye contact with one another and focus on the speaker. If you can't put them in a circle, coach students to turn and look at the person who is speaking.

Establish general discussion guidelines with the group. A few suggestions:

- Look at the person who is speaking.

- Focus on what the person is saying rather than on your own thoughts.

- Keep your hands and body as still as you can, and turn in the direction of the person who is speaking.

- Don't interrupt or raise your hand when someone else is speaking.

- Allow people the right to opinions and feelings that differ from your own.

For some of the discussions, you may want to pass an object around the circle and have each person speak as they hold it. That way, everybody gets drawn in.

If one student tends to dominate, talk to that person privately and stress the importance of allowing time for others to speak. In addition, coax the quieter students to share. Let them know that what they think and feel is important.

The sessions will be most powerful when related to the experiences of the students. Ask open-ended questions to encourage this kind of sharing:

- **How did you feel when ...?**

- **What thoughts did you have about ...?**

- **How do you think this person felt when you ...?**

- **If you were this person, how might you have been feeling?**

- **What ideas came up for you when ...?**

As much as possible, relate the activities and questions back to the students' own lives. The leader's guide gives you many strategies for doing this.

Anticipating Challenges

Resistant students. Some students will say, "I like to fight," especially those who have been exposed to violence. Try not to judge, but rather appeal to their highest selves, the part that exists under the tough exterior. Be open to the possibility that resistant kids may change their outlooks over time. Be patient, and keep believing in them.

Children in extreme need. Students who are living with continuous conflict, neglect, or abuse may need extra attention from you. The sessions may bring up sensitive issues for them. If that happens, connect them to a guidance counselor or school nurse. Familiarize yourself with community services available. Any child who needs someone to talk to can call the National Youth Crisis Hotline (1-800-448-4663). In addition, leaders must follow the school's or organization's policy guidelines on mandatory reporting of physical or sexual abuse.

Students who struggle with writing. Notebook writing, surveys, interviews, and other written exercises are featured throughout this book. If a student has difficulty writing or resists doing so, consider having him or her tape record a written assignment. Another option is dictation—there may be a family adult or friend who is willing to write or type the student's words. As an alternative, a young person can dialogue with a trusted friend or family member instead of writing. The student can then report back to the class about what was discussed.

Deep Breathing

Early on, students will be introduced to deep abdominal breathing, one of the most important strategies for calming oneself and regaining self-control (see pages 71–72 in *The Kids' Guide*). Teach it with care and use it often with the group. When I was teaching, I would start many sessions by asking students to take deep breaths together. I would also use breathing during transitions—when students entered the room, switched from one activity to the next, or any time they got restless. It never ceased to amaze me how this simple technique would help kids refocus, especially those who had emotional issues or attention problems. Through continued practice, students will start integrating abdominal breathing into their lives and will use it more readily when faced with conflict and anger.

Getting Started

1. Read *The Kids' Guide to Working Out Conflicts.*

2. Read through the Preface and Introduction of the leader's guide (pages ix–x and 1–5) and review each session before teaching it. If possible, try a few of the recommended exercises yourself.

3. Make copies of one of the notes to family adults (pages 7 and 8) and distribute it to each student. Ask students to take the letters home to their family adults, so the adults can know about the young person's participation in learning conflict resolution and can be supportive of it. I've included two letters—one for use in a school setting (page 7), the other for use in a youth group or an organization (page 8). Adapt the wording to your own needs.

4. Assemble materials:

• Students will need a copy of *The Kids' Guide to Working Out Conflicts*, a notebook, a pen or pencil, and a pocket folder to store surveys, checklists, and logs.

• For most of the sessions you will need chart paper or a board to write on. Posting the charts in the classroom is a great way to reinforce the concepts in this guide. If you end up with too many charts, hang some in the hallways.

Evaluating Students' Learning

If you wish to measure students' progress throughout the sessions, you can use the "What I've Learned About Working Out Conflicts" quizzes (which correspond to the eight steps in *The Kids' Guide*) and the final summary test (which reviews all the steps) provided in the Supplemental Materials on pages 93–102. The answer key for the quizzes and test is on pages 103–105.

Using *The Kids' Guide to Working Out Conflicts* and *The Leader's Guide* Together

Kids' Guide	Pages	Leader's Guide	Pages
Step 1: Open Your Mind	1–5	**Session 1:** Why Learn to Resolve Conflicts?	11
	6–10	**Session 2:** What Starts a Conflict? What Makes It Grow?	14
	11–15	**Session 3:** Willingness Is the Key	17
	15–18	**Session 4:** Basement or Balcony—Making the Choice	19
Step 2: Decide to Become a Conflict Solver	20–25	**Session 5:** Using "Stop, Breathe, Chill" to Solve Conflicts	22
	25–28	**Session 6:** The Dignity Stance: Taking a Peaceful Stand	26
	28–34	**Session 7:** Learning from Conflict Solvers	31
Step 3: Become a Better Listener	36–43	**Session 8:** Listening to Help Solve Conflicts	33
	43–49	**Session 9:** How to Spark a Turnaround	37
Step 4: Use Win/Win Guidelines	50–56	**Session 10:** Using I-Messages	40
	57–60	**Session 11:** The Win/Win Guidelines: Taking Responsibility to Help Resolve Conflicts	44
	60–65	**Session 12:** The Win/Win Guidelines: Brainstorming Solutions and Affirming the Other Person	47
	65–67	**Session 13:** Applying the Win/Win Guidelines to Real-Life Conflicts	50
Step 5: Manage Your Anger and Gain Control	68–74	**Session 14:** Understanding and Gaining Control of Your Anger	53
	75–80	**Session 15:** Becoming Zinger-Proof	56
	80–83	**Session 16:** Using Visualization to Stay Cool	58
Step 6: Learn to Manage Stress and Stay Calm, Cool, and Confident	84–88	**Session 17:** Coping with Stress	60
	88–91	**Session 18:** Peaceful Place Visualization	63
	91–98	**Session 19:** The Secret of 5/25	66
Step 7: Be Smart About Bullying	99–104	**Session 20:** Dealing with Teasing	68
	104–108	**Session 21:** Standing Up for Someone Who Is Being Bullied	70
	108–117	**Session 22:** Responding to Being Bullied	74
Step 8: Build Yourself Up from the Inside Out	119–121	**Session 23:** Spreading the Word About Working Out Conflicts	76
	121–126	**Session 24:** The Power of Forgiveness	78
	127–133	**Session 25:** Using a Day-by-Day Plan	81

Date: _____

Dear Family Adult,

Your student will soon be taking part in some exciting sessions on conflict resolution and peacemaking based on the book *The Kids' Guide to Working Out Conflicts: How to Keep Cool, Stay Safe, and Get Along* by Naomi Drew, M.A. The purpose of this book is to help preteens and teens learn how to talk out conflicts respectfully, become better listeners, resist violence, manage anger, and advocate for themselves and other kids.

We want our school to be a place where everyone feels safe and respected, and we want students to have the skills and confidence to resolve conflicts constructively. Along with other students, your student will be learning and practicing strategies that will help this happen. Students will be asked to apply the strategies at home, in school, and in the community.

You can help by asking your student what she or he is learning about conflict resolution and by discussing the ideas being covered in the sessions. Students will also be completing interviews, writing assignments, and other projects for homework. Some homework assignments suggest that students teach their families the skills and techniques they are learning. Please do all that you can to make time for your student to share these with you.

You may want to take a peek at *The Kids' Guide to Working Out Conflicts* yourself. The strategies in the book are appropriate for people of all ages and can be helpful for families, too.

Thank you for your support. If you have any questions, please feel free to contact me at _____.

Yours truly,

_____

Date: _____

Dear Family Adult,

Your child will soon be taking part in some exciting sessions on conflict resolution and peacemaking based on the book *The Kids' Guide to Working Out Conflicts: How to Keep Cool, Stay Safe, and Get Along* by Naomi Drew, M.A. The purpose of this book is to help preteens and teens learn how to talk out conflicts respectfully, become better listeners, resist violence, manage anger, and advocate for themselves and other kids.

We want to provide an environment where everyone feels safe and respected, and we want the young people in our program to have the skills and confidence to resolve conflicts constructively. As a group, we will be learning and practicing strategies that will help this happen. Students will be asked to apply the strategies here, at home, in school, and in the community.

You can help by asking your child what she or he is learning about conflict resolution and by discussing the ideas being covered in our group. Your child will also be completing interviews, writing assignments, and other outside projects. At times we'll suggest that the group teach their families the skills and techniques they are learning. Please do all that you can to make time for your child to share these with you.

You may want to take a peek at *The Kids' Guide to Working Out Conflicts* yourself. The strategies in the book are appropriate for people of all ages and can be helpful for families, too.

Thank you for your support. If you have any questions, please feel free to contact me at _____.

Yours truly,

_____

The Sessions

Why Learn to Resolve Conflicts?

(pages 1–5 in *The Kids' Guide to Working Out Conflicts*)

Note: Before the first session, establish ground rules with students. See pages 2–3 for guidance on how to do this.

Students will

- be introduced to *The Kids' Guide to Working Out Conflicts*
- explore attitudes about conflict
- discuss the concept of positive and negative choices in conflict

Materials

- chart paper and markers
- notebooks for students

- "Observing Conflict" handout (page 13), one per student

Preparation

- Divide a piece of chart paper into two columns. At the head of the first column write: **Negative Results of Bad Choices in Conflicts.** At the head of the second column write: **Positive Results of Good Choices in Conflicts.**
- Make copies of the "Observing Conflict" handout for each student.

1. Checking In (10 minutes)

Ask the group to define the word *conflict*. (Here's the definition: A conflict is a misunderstanding, disagreement, or fight between two or more people. It can also be something that goes on inside yourself, like, "Should I hang out with this person or that one?")

Write the definition on the chart paper. Ask students if they see many conflicts going on in their school or neighborhood. Can they describe some of the conflicts and what causes them? (Caution them not to use real names.) Discuss. Ask students: **Do you think conflict is normal?** Point out that it is, but the important thing is how we handle it.

Introduce *The Kids' Guide to Working Out Conflicts* and ask students to leaf through it. Explain that they'll be reading sections of it, discussing what they've read, and doing exercises together. Turn to page 1 and ask for volunteers to read some of the quotes from kids. Ask: **Which of these comments do you relate to the most? Why?** Discuss briefly.

2. Positive and Negative Choices in Conflict (25 minutes)

Turn the discussion to choices in conflict. Ask students: **Do you think it's possible for people to learn how to resolve conflicts peacefully?** Probe for their honest responses, whether positive or negative. You may want to share good and bad ways you've handled a conflict in your own life, to encourage the group to open up.

Pass out notebooks and have students divide a page into two columns with the following headings: "Negative Choices in Handling Conflict" and "Positive Choices in Handling Conflict." Have students work in small groups to brainstorm a list under each column. Circulate among the groups and give help where needed. (This can also be done as a large group activity if you prefer.)

When finished, ask students to share the choices they came up with. (*For example,* teasing, put-downs, and hitting will be common negative choices, as compared with cooling off, hearing out the other person, and talking things over.)

Shift the discussion. Ask the group for the short-term and long-term results of making negative choices. (*Short-term examples:* getting suspended for fighting, losing a friendship. *Long-term example:* ending up in trouble with the law.)

Then ask the group for the short-term and long-term results of making positive choices. (*Short-term example:* clearing up a misunderstanding that could have led to a physical fight. *Long-term example:* earning the trust of people by handling conflicts respectfully.)

On the prepared chart paper, record what the students came up with for the two columns. Discuss briefly.

Conclude by asking students: **Can you describe the difference between *reacting* to a conflict and *choosing* a response? Which is more likely to lead to a positive result? Why?**

3. Wrap-Up (10 minutes)

Write the following sentence on the chart paper and ask students to complete it (you can complete it also):

What I most want to learn about resolving conflicts is

_____.

Share your statement and ask students to share theirs. Compare and contrast the answers they give. Point out that *The Kids' Guide* will help them make positive choices when they are faced with conflict, so they can work things out peacefully with friends and family. Emphasize that change takes time and that you'll also be learning right along with them.

4. Looking Ahead

- Suggest that students decorate their notebooks with artwork or titles to express their personalities. Remind students to bring their notebooks to the next session.

- Assign the reading for Session 2: encourage students to read the introduction (pages 1–5), as well as pages 6–10 in *The Kids' Guide*.

- Tell students to complete the "Observing Conflict" handout for the next meeting.

 # Observing Conflict

Observe people in school. Look for conflicts in classrooms, the hallways, the cafeteria, or other places. Then fill out this form. (If you don't observe any conflicts, you can write about conflicts you had yourself or that you heard about from others.)

Make your own Top Five lists (if you can't list five, list as many as you can).

Top five things I noticed boys having conflicts over

1. _____
2. _____
3. _____
4. _____
5. _____

Top five things I noticed girls having conflicts over

1. _____
2. _____
3. _____
4. _____
5. _____

Three things people did to make the conflicts worse

1. _____
2. _____
3. _____

Three things people did to solve the conflicts peacefully

1. _____
2. _____
3. _____

Was there a better way people could have handled the conflicts I saw? Write about it here:

_____

_____

_____

What Starts a Conflict? What Makes It Grow?

(pages 6–10 in *The Kids' Guide to Working Out Conflicts*)

Students will

- review ground rules for the sessions
- gain insight into what triggers conflicts and what makes them grow
- understand the three elements required to work out conflicts

Materials

- chart paper and markers
- completed "Observing Conflict" handouts from Session 1
- "My Conflict Triggers" handout (page 16), one per student

Preparation

- On a piece of chart paper, make the following sign:

  Working Out Conflicts Requires . . .
  1. A desire to change.
  2. The willingness to try something new.
  3. Patient determination, also known as perseverance.

- Make copies of the "My Conflict Triggers" handout for each student.

1. Checking In (5 minutes)

Welcome students back. Review the ground rules that you established with the group at the beginning of Session 1. Discuss any questions or concerns students have about the rules. Stress the importance of working together in an atmosphere of safety.

2. Observing Conflict (25 minutes)

Have students take out the "Observing Conflict" handouts they completed. (If some students didn't observe a conflict, they can discuss a conflict they had or heard about.)

Ask students: **What were the Top Five things you noticed boys having conflicts over? How about girls? How were the two groups alike in the kinds of conflicts they had? How were they different?** List students' answers on the chart paper and discuss.

Then ask the group: **What did you observe people saying or doing that made conflicts worse?** List on the chart paper and discuss.

Refer students to the introduction of *The Kids' Guide* and ask: **What three things listed there are necessary for working out conflicts?** Give them time to answer, then show the sign:

> Working Out Conflicts Requires . . .
> 1. A desire to change.
> 2. The willingness to try something new.
> 3. Patient determination, also known as perseverance.

Ask the group: **Why do you think people are sometimes unwilling to work out conflicts peacefully?** Refer students back to the conflicts they observed. **Did more people make the conflict worse or handle it peacefully? What stood in the way of a peaceful solution? Was there a better way to handle the conflicts? How? What ways did you observe people handling conflicts peacefully?**

Turn to page 9 of *The Kids' Guide* and ask volunteers to take turns reading the quotes about conflict triggers at the top of the page. Ask students which comments they relate to and why. What kinds of things trigger their conflicts?

3. Wrap-Up (10 minutes)

Refer to Thanh's story at the top of page 8 of *The Kid's Guide.* Ask a student to read it aloud. Then ask the group:

- **Why was Thanh angry?**
- **Can you think of a time when a bad mood triggered a conflict?**
- **Did Thanh choose his response or just react?**

- **What might Thanh have said or done differently?**
- **What other choices did he have?**

List the choices students suggest on the chart paper. Emphasize that *choosing* a response usually leads to more positive results than *reacting.* Discuss the difference between the two. Tell the group that they will be learning more about what triggers their responses and new ways to choose how to respond.

Thank students for their participation and acknowledge their contributions.

4. Looking Ahead

- Tell the group you want to end each session with a slogan, song, quote, or rap that they like or have made up themselves. Tell students to bring these to the next session.

- Assign the reading for Session 3: pages 11–15 of *The Kids' Guide.*

- Ask students to complete the "My Conflict Triggers" handout.

Additional Activities (Instructions for Students)

Top 10 Conflict Starters at Home. In your notebook, list the top ten conflict starters in your home. The conflicts can be with other kids in the home or with adults. Then answer this question: "How do I play a part in contributing to the conflicts?"

Moods and Conflict. Observe your moods at home and in school. Do you sometimes find yourself getting grouchy with the people around you? Notice what you do and say when you're feeling irritable or grouchy. Notice your body language and facial expressions, too. Write about them in your notebook. What can you do to help avoid conflicts when you're in a bad mood? Brainstorm at least three ideas.

 # My Conflict Triggers

Most of my conflicts are with: _____

They usually happen because: _____

_____

What this person does that bothers me most: _____

_____

When she/he does this, here's how I usually feel: _____

Then here's what I usually do: _____

_____

And then he/she does this: _____

_____

If my best friend were having this conflict, I would offer this advice: _____

_____

Next time a conflict with this person is possible, here's something I can do to make the conflict better: ____

_____

_____

I also have conflicts with: _____

They usually happen because: _____

_____

What this person does that bothers me most: _____

_____

When she/he does this, here's how I usually feel: _____

Then here's what I usually do: _____

_____

And then he/she does this: _____

_____

If my best friend were having this conflict, I would offer this advice: _____

_____

_____

Next time a conflict with this person is possible, here's something I can do to make the conflict better: ____

_____

_____

Willingness Is the Key

(pages 11–15 in *The Kids' Guide to Working Out Conflicts*)

Students will

- gain more insight into their conflict triggers
- understand that willingness is critical to working out conflicts
- identify their willingness blocks

Materials

- completed "My Conflict Triggers" handouts from Session 2
- chart paper and markers
- a building block or a picture of one

- "Negative Results of Bad Choices in Conflicts" and "Positive Results of Good Choices in Conflicts" chart from Session 1
- "Working Out Conflicts Requires . . ." sign from Session 2

Preparation

- You'll need an actual block for this session, for example, a children's building block. (You can also use a drawing or photograph of a block, or ask a student to draw a block prior to this session.)

1. Checking In (15 minutes)

Welcome students back. Have students take out the "My Conflict Triggers" handouts they completed. Lead a discussion of the various ways conflicts are triggered by asking the following questions:

- **What did you discover about your triggers? What caused you to get into a conflict?** (List students' triggers on the chart paper.)

- **How did you react when someone triggered you?**

- **Did your reaction bring about a positive or negative result? Why?**

Ask if anyone was able to choose a response rather than just react. If so, what did they choose to do? Can they think of what enabled them to make a choice, rather than just react? (*For example*, taking a step back, thinking before speaking, remembering something they read in the book or talked about in class.)

During the discussion, look for similarities among students in what triggers their conflicts (*for instance*, feeling annoyed by someone, not liking the other person, feeling taken advantage of).

2. Role-Playing Actual Conflicts (20 minutes)

Ask for two volunteers to act out an actual conflict a student experienced. Confer with the two students briefly to review how they will act out the role play (see pages 3–4 for complete guidance on how to conduct role plays).

After the role play, ask the actors: **Were you choosing responses to one another or simply reacting? What were your willingness blocks?** (*For example*, wanting to be right, wanting to win rather than compromise, wanting to hurt the other person.) As the blocks are identified, hand the actual block or picture of it to each actor.

Then ask the larger group to react to the role play as you list their responses to the first question on the chart paper: **What could the actors have done differently to have ended up with a more positive outcome? Was there a place where the conflict escalated?** (Write the word "escalate" on the chart paper. Ask for the meaning of the word and write it down, too.) **What caused the conflict to escalate? What could the actors have done differently to resolve the conflict in a positive way?**

3. Wrap-Up (10 minutes)

Refer students to page 13 of *The Kids' Guide:* "I'd like to stop having conflicts, BUT sometimes (or often) . . . " Pass the block to a few people and ask them to identify which items on the list they most relate to. Ask the students: **Is it worth it to hold onto this block? Do you think you could give up the block? Why or why not?**

To end the session, ask for volunteers to share a slogan, song, quote, or rap.

4. Looking Ahead

• Assign the reading for Session 4: pages 15–18 in *The Kid's Guide.*

• Remind students to bring in more slogans, songs, quotes, or raps for the next session.

Additional Activities (Instructions for Students)

Confronting Willingness Blocks. Observe yourself with people and notice when you're willing to work out conflicts and when you're not. What gets in the way? Think about what your willingness blocks are in each situation. Write about this in your notebook. Ask yourself what you can do differently when you notice your willingness blocks coming up. Write about this, too. Now write about how your life could be different if you let go of some of your willingness blocks.

"A Time I Was Unwilling to Work Out a Conflict, and Why." Write about this topic using a technique called *automatic writing* to help you spur ideas—write for about two minutes without stopping, allowing ideas to flow freely. Neatness, spelling, and grammar do not count. The purpose of writing without stopping is to unlock what's beneath the surface and have it revealed on paper. If you wish, share what you write with the group.

Basement or Balcony—Making the Choice

(pages 15–18 in *The Kids' Guide to Working Out Conflicts*)

Students will

- review willingness blocks
- learn how to work out a conflict with a resistant person
- learn about the basement or balcony concept

Materials

- chart paper and markers
- "Working Out Conflicts Requires . . ." sign from Session 3
- "Basement or Balcony" handout (page 21), one per student

Preparation

- Make copies of the "Basement or Balcony" handout for each student.

1. Checking In (10 minutes)

Welcome students back. Ask about their reactions to what they read in *The Kids' Guide* since the last session. Ask about their reactions to the sessions so far: **What do you like? What could be improved? What do you want to learn about in future sessions?** Make adjustments as necessary. (From time to time, continue checking in about students' reactions to the sessions.)

2. Basement or Balcony? (25 minutes)

Ask the group: **Do you think it's possible to work out a conflict if the other person isn't willing?** Discuss. **Has anyone ever solved a conflict with an unwilling person? What did they do to resolve it?** Share your own experiences.

Be prepared that many students won't think it's possible to resolve a conflict with an unwilling person. The answer, however, is "yes," and explain to the group that they will be learning ways to resolve conflicts with people who aren't willing.

Ask for two volunteers to act out the following role play: *Todd and Jamal sit next to each other in math class. Todd gets up to get an eraser. When he returns to his seat, Jamal is using the calculator that belongs to Todd. Todd immediately gets mad.*

Tell the volunteers that both Todd and Jamal are unwilling to work out the conflict peacefully. Caution them ahead of time that they are not allowed to physically touch one another.

After the role play, ask the group: **What did you see happening? What caused the conflict to escalate?** Ask about tone of voice, facial expression, and body language, as well as the words spoken. **What could Todd and Jamal have done to prevent a negative outcome to their conflict?**

Have students form pairs. Ask them to brainstorm what choices either Todd or Jamal could have made to settle the conflict peacefully and maturely. Have the pairs share their ideas with the group. Ask the group: **What might prevent you from making such choices?** Discuss.

Turn to pages 15–16 of *The Kids' Guide:* "Hey—That's Mine!" Ask for two volunteers to act out the conflict between Todd and Jamal. (They can read from the book as they do the role play.) After the role play, ask the group: **Was Jamal in the basement or balcony during the conflict?** (Balcony.) **Where was Todd?** (Basement.)

Ask the group to define the difference between the basement and the balcony in a conflict. Next, see if students can pinpoint the moment in the conflict when Jamal could have easily been drawn into the basement but refused to do so. (When Todd reaches for the calculator.) Ask the group:

- **Why can it be difficult to go to the balcony like Jamal did?**

- **What is the benefit of choosing the balcony over the basement?**

3. Wrap-Up (10 minutes)

Ask the group to name all the things Jamal did when Todd wasn't willing to work out the conflict. The list should include:

- Used a calm tone of voice.

- Put the calculator on the table instead of holding onto it.

- Took a deep breath when Todd gave him a hard time.

- Steadied his voice when he needed to.

- Continued speaking in a respectful manner.

- Used reasoning.

- Listened to what Todd had to say.

- Refrained from arguing or blaming.

- Didn't let Todd's resistant attitude suck him into negative behavior.

- Worked toward a fair solution.

Ask students for suggestions of additional things someone can do to resolve a conflict when the other person isn't willing. Conclude by reminding students that they always have the power to *choose* their responses in a conflict and not just *react.*

4. Looking Ahead

- Assign the reading for Session 5: pages 20–25 in *The Kids' Guide.*

- Ask students to complete the "Basement or Balcony" handout for the next session.

Additional Activity (Instructions for Students)

Deciding to Be Better. Read the following quote from page 18 of *The Kids' Guide:* "I watch people be mean to each other. I've decided to be better than that." In your notebook, write about what this means to you. How could you apply this idea to your own life?

Basement or Balcony:
Which Did You Choose?

Observe yourself when you're involved in conflicts over the next two days. Then fill out the sections below.

Conflict 1

Description of the conflict: _____

_____

What I did in response to the conflict: _____

_____

Where did I go—basement or balcony? _____

_____

If I went to the basement, what made me end up there? _____

_____

If I went to the balcony, how did I manage to stay there? _____

_____

If the conflict ended in a negative way, what can I do differently next time? _____

_____

_____

_____

Conflict 2

Description of the conflict: _____

_____

What I did in response to the conflict: _____

_____

Where did I go—basement or balcony? _____

_____

If I went to the basement, what made me end up there? _____

_____

If I went to the balcony, how did I manage to stay there? _____

_____

If the conflict ended in a negative way, what can I do differently next time? _____

_____

_____

_____

Using "Stop, Breathe, Chill" to Solve Conflicts

(pages 20–25 in *The Kids' Guide to Working Out Conflicts*)

Note: Leaders should read pages 70–75 in *The Kids' Guide*, which explains the "Stop, Breathe, Chill" technique in detail, and keep that section handy as a reference during this session.

Students will

- learn more about their basement or balcony reactions to conflict
- be introduced to the "Stop, Breathe, Chill" calming technique
- understand the difference between conflict solvers and conflict makers

Materials

- chart paper and markers
- completed "Basement or Balcony" handouts from Session 4

- "When I Have a Conflict" handout (page 24), one per student
- "Conflict Log" handout, (page 25), three per student

Preparation

- On chart paper, write the following sentence:

  "When there's a conflict, the choices you make at each moment determine the outcome."

- On another sheet of chart paper, prepare the following sign (you can ask a student to draw a small illustration next to each word):

  STOP   BREATHE   CHILL

- Make copies of the "When I Have a Conflict" and "Conflict Log" handouts for each student.

1. Checking In (10 minutes)

Have students take out their completed "Basement or Balcony" handouts. Ask: **What did you learn from completing the handout? Did you spend more time in the basement or balcony? Why? What made it difficult to go to the balcony and stay there? Why did you end up in the basement? What could help you go to the balcony more often?**

2. "Stop, Breathe, Chill" Gives You the Power to Solve Conflicts (30 minutes)

Ask a volunteer to read aloud the sentence on the chart: "When there's a conflict, the choices you make at each moment determine the outcome." Ask the group what it means and how it applies to conflicts they've had. How does it relate to the difference between choosing and reacting?

Now ask two volunteers to role-play "'Oops!': Scene 3" on page 23 of *The Kids' Guide*. After the role play, ask the group:

- **Who was the conflict solver in this scene?** (Ramón.)

- **What did Ramón do to resolve the conflict peacefully, even though Al was acting negatively?** (He chose his actions instead of just reacting.)

- **Do you think you could do what Ramón did? Why or why not?** (For kids who say "no," ask what would prevent them from doing so. Encourage the group to discuss these fears.)

- **What technique did Ramón use to calm himself when Al called him an idiot?** ("Stop, Breathe, Chill.")

Tell the group they are going to learn the technique Ramón used to keep his cool (see pages 70–75 of *The Kids' Guide*).

Take plenty of time teaching the breathing part of this technique. Have students practice it with you. Make sure they inhale slowly into the lower abdomen, hold the breath for a few seconds, then release it slowly. Do this with the group at least three times.

Then ask the group about other things that Ramón did to keep his cool. (He repeated a calming statement to himself: "You can handle this without losing your cool.") Ask the group for suggestions of calming statements they can say to themselves when faced with a conflict. They should be brief and positive, and should start with "I," such as:

- "I can keep my cool."

- "I can resolve this without fighting."

List the calming statements on chart paper.

Ask for two volunteers to role-play a conflict, preferably a real conflict one of the students had. The first student should try to escalate the conflict. The second student should use "Stop, Breathe, Chill" and calming statements to prevent the conflict from escalating.

After the role play, ask the first actor how it felt to try to escalate the conflict when the other person used "Stop, Breathe, Chill." Ask the second actor how it felt to use "Stop, Breathe, Chill" when the other person wanted to escalate the conflict.

Then ask the larger group for their responses to the role play: **Can you see using "Stop, Breathe, Chill" in a real conflict? Can you see it helping you go to the balcony rather than the basement? Why or why not?**

To conclude, have the students write down a calming statement in their notebooks that they will use the next time they're faced with a conflict.

3. Wrap-Up (5 minutes)

End with a slogan, song, quote, or rap that the students have come up with.

4. Looking Ahead

- Pass out the "When I Have a Conflict" handout (one per student) and the "Conflict Log" handouts (three per student). Ask the students to fill them out before the next session.

- Assign the reading for Session 6: pages 25–28 of *The Kids' Guide*.

Additional Activities (Instructions for Students)

Feelings and Thoughts We Have in Conflicts. Do the "Try It" activity on page 23 of *The Kids' Guide*. In your notebook, write about the feelings you have and the thoughts you think the next time you're in a conflict. Create a calming statement you can use to counter the negative thoughts that come up.

Managing Anger Activity. Make a sign to hang up at home with the words "STOP, BREATHE, CHILL." Tell your family about this technique. Use it when you're at home.

When I Have a Conflict

You may have heard teachers or other kids talk about conflict resolution. This is another term for solving or resolving conflicts. When it comes to conflict resolution, where do you stand right now? What are you doing to be a conflict solver? Take this quick self-test to find out. Respond yes or no to each statement:

When I have a conflict . . .

_____ I try to calm down before I react.

_____ I do my best to avoid physical fighting.

_____ I believe I have more to gain by working things out.

_____ I listen to what the other person has to say.

_____ I try to see how I'm responsible instead of just blaming the other person.

_____ I look for ways to solve the problem rather than win the argument.

_____ I'm willing to compromise.

_____ I avoid using put-downs.

_____ I speak my truth, but I do it respectfully.

_____ I try to put myself in the other person's place instead of only focusing on my own stuff.

How many times did you answer yes?

Five or more? If so, you're already a conflict solver a good part of the time. Keep at it! Also know that you'll become an even better conflict solver by working to turn your "no" answers into "yeses."

Fewer than five? You're not there yet . . . but you can get there. Choose one new idea to try and do it until it starts to come more easily. Then choose another. Also continue doing whatever you said yes to.

If you answered yes to the third statement, you've already made an important start. As you read earlier, being willing to work out conflicts is the first big step on the road to becoming a conflict solver.

Conflict Log

Date: _____

Here's who I had a conflict with: _____

What triggered it? _____

_____

How did I react? _____

_____

Did my actions make the conflict better or worse? _____

_____

How did the conflict end? _____

_____

Did I go to the basement? The balcony? A little of both? _____

_____

Here's how I feel about the way things turned out: _____

_____

_____

_____

If my best friend had the same conflict, what would I have told him or her
to do? _____

_____

What could I have done differently? _____

_____

_____

_____

When could I have stopped and taken some breaths to regain control? _____

_____

_____

What could I have told myself in order to calm down? _____

_____

_____

What is one thing I did today, or can do tomorrow, to help me stay calm and in control during a
conflict? _____

_____

The Dignity Stance: Taking a Peaceful Stand

(pages 25–28 in *The Kids' Guide to Working Out Conflicts*)

Students will

- understand what to do in a conflict when someone is verbally aggressive
- learn to use the Dignity Stance to avoid conflict
- understand how to act assertively, not aggressively

Materials

- chart paper and markers
- completed "Conflict Logs" from Session 5
- "Conflict Solver Interview" handout (page 29), one per student
- "Dignity Stance" handout (page 30), one per student

Preparation

- Make copies of the "Dignity Stance" and "Conflict Solver Interview" handouts for each student.
- On chart paper, write the following:

Dignity Stance
- Stand tall with your head held high.
- Make direct eye contact.
- Use a firm, steady tone of voice.
- Be aware of your body language and facial expression.
- When you walk away, do it with pride.

- Make extra copies of the "Conflict Log" handout (page 25) for students who may need them.

1. Checking In (10 minutes)

Discuss what students learned by filling out the "When I Have a Conflict" and "Conflict Log" handouts, asking questions like:

- **What triggered a conflict you had?**

- **Did your reactions make the conflict better or worse? Why?**

- **What could you do differently the next time to stay calm and in control during an argument or fight?**

Tell students that today they will learn a new technique for handling conflict while also standing up for themselves.

2. Standing Up for Yourself Peacefully: The Dignity Stance (30 minutes)

Lead a discussion on the difference between being assertive and being aggressive. Ask students to define the difference between the two. (Assertive means speaking your mind with respect, aggressive means ready to argue or fight.) List the definitions on chart paper. Give an example.

Ask the group: **How can being assertive help you avoid fights?** This may be a difficult concept to understand at first. Being assertive means you can face someone who wants to fight, but you are brave and confident enough to walk away from it. Being aggressive usually escalates a conflict. Remind the group of the importance of choosing a reaction so a conflict doesn't escalate.

Tell students that they're going to learn how to walk away from conflicts and come across as strong and brave (as opposed to wimpy and scared). It's called the Dignity Stance and you will teach it to them in a little while. But first, tell them that practicing the breathing part of "Stop, Breathe, Chill" will make it easier for them to use the Dignity Stance when they're in conflicts.

Spend a few moments practicing abdominal breathing with the students, reminding them to say a calming statement to themselves as they breathe. Make sure they inhale slowly into the lower abdomen and then slowly exhale. Have them do the breathing at least three times.

Hold up the chart outlining the Dignity Stance. Go over it with the group. Ask a volunteer to read aloud "'I Hear You've Been Talking': Scene 1" on pages 25–26 of *The Kids' Guide.* Ask the group:

• **What did Lyla do to prevent the conflict from escalating into a fight?**

• **Can you name all of the actions Lyla took that enabled her to keep her cool?**

List the actions on chart paper under the heading "Standing Up for Yourself Assertively." Make sure all of the following are included.

• Breathed deeply when she felt anger or fear.

• Said a calming statement to herself.

• Didn't make faces or roll her eyes.

• Stood tall without looking threatening.

• Wasn't sarcastic.

• Listened to what was being said.

• Did not react impulsively.

• Walked away tall and proud.

Ask students to think of a conflict they had when the person was verbally aggressive toward them. They can refer to real conflicts from their "Conflict Logs." Have two volunteers act it out. One student should try to escalate the conflict. The other student should be assertive and use "Stop, Breathe, Chill" and the Dignity Stance.

When the role play is over, ask the group what they observed the assertive person doing. Draw attention to the importance of body language—kids will often make faces or roll their eyes without even realizing it. The same goes for hands on hips, crossing the arms, and so forth. Help build students' awareness of these behaviors and how they can escalate conflicts.

Ask the two actors:

• **How did it feel to use the Dignity Stance during the role play? Did you feel in control and able to avoid the conflict?**

• **How did it feel to try to escalate the conflict when your partner was using the Dignity Stance? Did it make it harder for you to keep the conflict going?**

If there is time, conduct a second role play.

3. Wrap-Up (5 minutes)

Close with a slogan, song, quote, or rap the group has come up with.

4. Looking Ahead

• Hand out copies of the Dignity Stance. Ask students to tape the handouts into their notebooks. Suggest that they practice the stance at home in the mirror.

• Tell students to continue filling out their "Conflict Logs" until they complete three of them. Remind them to use "Stop, Breathe, Chill" and the Dignity Stance the next time a conflict arises. In their notebooks, ask them to write about any changes they notice in how they're handling conflicts and what happens when they use the techniques just mentioned.

• Ask students to complete the "Conflict Solver Interview" handout.

• Assign the reading for Session 7: pages 28–34 of *The Kids' Guide*.

Additional Activity (Instructions for Students)

Managing Anger Visualization Activity. Tonight, as you're laying in bed before falling asleep, practice the deep breathing you learned about in class. Then think of a conflict you had that ended negatively. Replay the conflict in your head, this time picturing yourself using "Stop, Breathe, Chill" and the Dignity Stance. Imagine the conflict ending in a positive way. In the morning, write about what you pictured in your mind.

 # Conflict Solver Interview

Choose someone who you think is good at handling or solving conflicts. This person gets along well with others, works out problems fairly, and stands up for himself or herself, but does so respectfully. Ask this person the following questions and write the answers below.

1. What do you do to calm down when someone says or does something that gets you mad?

_____

_____

_____

_____

_____

2. What do you do to avoid using put-downs when you're in a conflict?

_____

_____

_____

_____

_____

3. How do you manage to work out conflicts without fighting?

_____

_____

_____

_____

_____

4. Is there something you say to yourself that helps you keep your cool in conflict situations?

_____

_____

_____

_____

_____

5. What advice do you have for other people when it comes to handling conflict?

_____

_____

_____

_____

_____

Dignity Stance

Stand tall with your head held high.

Make direct eye contact.

Use a firm, steady tone of voice.

Be aware of your body language and facial expression.

When you walk away, do it with pride.

Learning from Conflict Solvers

(pages 28–34 in *The Kids' Guide to Working Out Conflicts*)

Dr. Martin Luther King Jr.

Note: You may want to devote additional sessions just to this topic, including role plays of actual conflicts that ended up as fights, and how kids can walk away if they find themselves in the same situation.

Students will

- gain insight into what conflict solvers do when faced with a conflict
- learn to practice these techniques
- learn how to use exit lines to walk away from a conflict with dignity

Materials

- chart paper and markers
- completed "Conflict Logs" from previous sessions
- completed "Conflict Solver Interviews" from Session 6
- "Dignity Stance" chart from Session 6
- "Standing Up for Yourself Assertively" chart from Session 6

Preparation

- Make additional copies of "Conflict Logs" for kids who may need them.

1. Checking In (5 minutes)

Have students take out their completed "Conflict Logs." (By now each student should have filled out three pages.) Ask: **Did anyone use "Stop, Breathe, Chill" and the Dignity Stance to peacefully settle a conflict? What success or difficulties did you have in handling conflicts? What changes, if any, are you noticing in the way you handle conflict?**

2. Learning from Conflict Solvers (25 minutes)

Have students take out their completed "Conflict Solver Interviews." Go around the room and ask each student to name one positive thing they learned from the person about working out conflicts peacefully. How does the person stay calm and avoid acting aggressively? How does the person avoid physical fights? On chart paper, list what students learned from the interviews.

Ask a volunteer to read aloud page 29 of *The Kids' Guide*, "Whose Shirt Is That?" Ask the group: **In addition to the Dignity Stance, what else did Andi do to avoid getting hooked by Jaquie's negative comment? How did Andi prevent this situation from turning into a fight? If you saw this happening for real, how would you feel about the way Andi handled herself?**

Now ask a volunteer to read aloud "Real Words from the Survey" from page 29 of *The Kids' Guide:* "Sometimes the brave kids just walk away. Sometimes the *un*brave kids fight and try to show off." Ask students:

- **Why does it take courage to walk away from a fight? Would you do it? Why or why not?**

- **What's the difference between walking away weak and scared, and walking away with your head held high?** (Remind students of the Dignity Stance.)

Make it clear to students that being a conflict solver doesn't mean letting people beat you up or make you look foolish. What it does mean is using every option available other than fighting, when you can. In some cases—if we are in real danger—we have to fight to defend ourselves. But that is usually the exception rather than the rule.

Ask the group to come up with exit lines—short responses they can make when someone teases them or challenges them to a fight. *For example:*

- "This isn't worth fighting over."

- "Hey, man, let's chill."

- "I hear you and I understand."

- "It's not worth getting in trouble over."

List the students' ideas on a chart titled "Exit Lines."

Conduct a role play where one student challenges the other to a fight. It can be a real conflict the student experienced. Have the person who is challenged use the Dignity Stance and one of the exit lines that's been suggested. In addition, make sure that the student who is challenged uses at least one thing he or she learned from the "Conflict Solver Interview." (Refer the student to the list the group created on chart paper if need be.)

After the role play, ask the group:

- **How did the Dignity Stance prevent the conflict from getting worse?**

- **How did the exit lines help?**

- **What did the student use from the "Conflict Solver Interview"? How did this help the student handle the conflict?**

- **Could you see yourself using these techniques? Why or why not?**

If there's time, conduct a second role play using new volunteers.

3. Wrap-Up (15 minutes)

Conduct an automatic writing exercise about walking away from a fight. Ask students to write as quickly as they can without lifting their hand from the page for about two minutes. Tell them not to worry about grammar or spelling, and that their work will not be collected. This approach is intended to get them to produce a free flow of feelings and ideas.

As they write, read aloud these writing prompts:

- **What can you do to walk away from a fight?**

- **What have you learned so far that can help you?**

- **What did you learn from the "Conflict Solver Interviews" that you could use?**

- **What other ideas can you come up with?**

- **What advice would you give to a friend about walking away from a fight?**

4. Looking Ahead

- Assign the reading for Session 8: pages 36–43 of *The Kids' Guide.*

- Ask students to continue thinking about ways to avoid physical fighting.

Listening to Help Solve Conflicts

(pages 36–43 in *The Kids' Guide to Working Out Conflicts*)

Students will

- learn the difference between good and bad listening
- understand that good listening is critical to resolving conflicts
- learn to apply the skills of good listening to resolving conflicts

Materials

- chart paper and markers
- "Check Out Your Listening" handout (page 35), one per student
- "What Good Listeners Do" handout (page 36), one per student

Preparation

- Make copies of the "Check Out Your Listening" and "What Good Listeners Do" handouts for each student.

1. Checking In (10 minutes)

Ask students how good listening skills can help work out conflicts (or how poor listening can make them worse). Have them give examples from their own lives. They can refer to their "Conflict Logs" again. Discuss some of the conflicts they had that were not resolved successfully. Did poor listening play a part? Discuss briefly.

Pass out the "Check Out Your Listening" handouts. Have students complete this self-assessment (you can complete it, too). Ask students: **What did you discover about your listening skills? What do you do well? What needs improvement?**

2. Using Good Listening in Conflict Situations (25 minutes)

Ask two volunteers to act out the "Bad Listening" role play on page 41 of *The Kids' Guide.* After the role play, ask students to name all the things they observed the bad listener do.

Now ask two new volunteers to act out the "Good Listening" role play on page 42 of *The Kids' Guide.* After the role play, ask how the second conversation differed from the first one. Ask students to name all the things the good listener did. List students' answers on chart paper under the heading "Good Listening." The list of good listening skills should include:

- Look at the person who is speaking and keep good eye contact.

- Lean in toward the speaker and nod to show that you're interested and that you're following what the person said.

- Think about what the speaker is saying.

- Don't interrupt.

- Stay focused on the speaker and don't let yourself be distracted.

- Ask questions to make sure you understand what the person means.

- Act like the speaker is the only person in the room.

If there's time, ask for two more volunteers to act out another conflict, using the elements of good listening to resolve it peacefully.

Conclude by asking students: **Do you think good listening skills can increase your personal power? How?** (See page 38 of *The Kids' Guide.*)

3. Wrap-Up (10 minutes)

Have students look at the "Check Out Your Listening" handouts they completed at the beginning of the session. Ask them to choose one or two listening goals for themselves to work on. (Or they can choose a goal from the "Good Listening" chart you made.) Ask for volunteers to share the goals they've chosen. Ask students: **Why did you choose this goal? Will it be difficult for you? Why?**

Ask students to work on these goals until the next session. Remind them about perseverance and that change takes time.

4. Looking Ahead

- Assign the reading for Session 9: pages 43–49 of *The Kids' Guide.*

- Ask students to complete the "What Good Listeners Do" handout.

Additional Activity (Instructions for Students)

Listening Power. Take a pledge to listen with focus and an open mind to everyone you interact with, for an entire day. Write about this experience in your notebook and be prepared to discuss it with the group.

 # Check Out Your Listening

How's your listening? Use this quiz for a quick self-check. Check each statement that applies to you.

When I listen...

_____ I make eye contact with the person who is speaking.

_____ I wait until the other person is finished before I start talking.

_____ I focus on what the speaker is saying instead of just thinking about what I'm going to say next.

_____ I hear the speaker out even if I don't agree with what I'm hearing.

_____ I don't hijack the conversation and make it about me.

_____ I care about what the other person has to say.

_____ I try to understand what the other person believes, feels, and wants.

_____ If there's a conflict, I listen to the other person's side of the story.

_____ I think it's important for people to listen to each other.

What Good Listeners Do

Spend some time talking to someone who you think is a good listener. After you talk to the person, fill out this form.

The person who's a great listener is: _____

Here are five things that person did when listening to me:

1. _____

2. _____

3. _____

4. _____

5. _____

When I'm around this person I feel: _____

_____

_____

Here's how other people respond to this person: _____

_____

_____

_____

Two things I noticed this person doing that I want to do to improve my listening are:

1. _____

2. _____

How to Spark a Turnaround

(pages 43–49 in *The Kids' Guide to Working Out Conflicts*)

Students will

- practice the skill of reflective listening
- use it to spark a turnaround in a conflict

Materials

- chart paper and markers
- completed "What Good Listeners Do" handouts from Session 8
- "Good Listening" chart from Session 8

Preparation

- On chart paper, make two signs:

Turnaround Point: The place in a conflict where we have the power to shift it from escalation to resolution.

To Spark a Turnaround: To choose actions that will cause a conflict to shift from escalation to resolution.

1. Checking In (10 minutes)

Ask students how they did on their listening goals from Session 8. Ask them: **What was hardest about changing the way you listened? What are you doing that's helping you listen better? Have you noticed a difference in the way you relate to people?**

Then review their "What Good Listeners Do" assignments. Go around the room and ask students to name one thing they learned from their

observations. Do they think they will be able to practice these listening skills themselves?

Tell the group that today they will learn more about good listening.

2. Using Reflective Listening to Spark a Turnaround (30 minutes)

Ask a volunteer to read aloud "'How Ya Doing?': Scene 2" on page 45 of *The Kids' Guide.*

Afterwards, ask students:

- **What triggered the conflict between Jeff and Mom?**

- **At what point did it escalate?**

- **How was Mom responsible?**

- **How was Jeff responsible?**

- **What could Jeff have done differently?** (He could have used a technique called *reflective listening* to turn the conflict around.)

Now have the group read "'How Ya Doing?': Scene 1" on page 44 of *The Kids' Guide.* Ask them what Jeff did differently in this scene.

Explain to students that reflective listening takes good listening a step further and that it can spark a turnaround in conflicts and prevent them from escalating.

Practice reflective listening with the group. Ask for a volunteer to reflect (say) back something you say. You could say, **"I can't wait until summer because my family and I will be taking a trip."** Coach the student who is reflecting back to start with the words, "I heard you say . . . ," "Sounds like . . . ," or "So you feel . . ." (*For example:* "Sounds like you're excited about summer because of the trip you and your family will be taking.")

Repeat this with a few students. Remind them that using reflective listening may feel awkward at first, but will feel more natural the more they do it.

Now introduce the concepts of "Turnaround Point" and "To Spark a Turnaround." Have volunteers read aloud the explanations on the signs. Ask the group:

- **What do these two phrases mean to you?**

- **How do they relate to conflicts you've had?**

- **Why do you think it's important to know how and when to turn around a conflict?**

Now ask volunteers to act out a real-life conflict. Direct the first student to start the conflict and the second student to use reflective listening to turn the conflict around. Ask the group for additional strategies the second student can use to work out the conflict (*for example,* deep breathing, calming statement, and being aware of body language, facial expression, tone of voice). List students' suggestions on the chart paper.

Conduct the role play.

If the conflict turns around and is resolved, ask students:

- **What was the turnaround point? At what place in the conflict did it take place?**

- **What did the second student do to spark the turnaround?**

Ask the student who sparked the turnaround:

- **What did you do to keep your cool?**

- **How did it feel to use reflective listening?**

- **What thoughts did you think to keep yourself calm?**

- **How did it feel to remain in control of your actions and words and to spark a turnaround?**

If the conflict escalates instead of turning around, ask the group to identify what went wrong. Did the second student fail to use reflective listening? Did she or he act defensively or send out any aggressive messages? What could the person do differently the next time to spark a turnaround?

3. Wrap-Up (5 minutes)

End with a slogan, song, quote, or rap the students have made up.

4. Looking Ahead

- Assign the reading for Session 10: pages 50–56 of *The Kids' Guide.*

- Ask students to use reflective listening at home and to play "I Heard You Say" with their families. Next time students get into a conflict, they can try saying back what they heard (in a neutral way) instead of arguing. Ask students to write about the conflict in their notebooks.

OPEN A BOOK

OPEN YOUR MIND

1-800-735-7323

free spirit
PUBLiSHiNG®

Helping kids
help themselves™
since 1983

www.freespirit.com

If you liked this book, you'll also like

- ### *What Do You Stand For?*

  Young people need guidance from caring adults to build strong, positive character traits—but they can also build their own. This inspiring book invites them to explore and practice honesty, kindness, empathy, integrity, tolerance, patience, respect, and more. For ages 11 & up.

- ### *Knowing Me, Knowing You* and *A Leader's Guide to Knowing Me, Knowing You*

  Using the DiSC® dimensions of behavior (direct and active, interested and lively, steady and cooperative, concerned and correct), teens learn how their personal styles change from one situation to the next and explore ways to use this knowledge for more effective interactions with others. For ages 12 & up.

WHAT DO YOU
STAND FOR?
A Kid's Guide
to Building Character

1-57542-029-5, $19.95

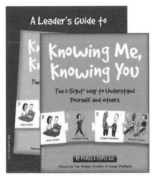

KNOWING ME,
KNOWING YOU
The I-Sight® Way
to Understand
Yourself and
Others

A LEADER'S
GUIDE TO
KNOWING ME,
KNOWING YOU

Kids book: 1-57542-090-2, $13.95
Leader's guide: 1-57542-091-0, $21.95

Call 1-800-735-7323 to order or mail this card for a FREE catalog!

Send me a Free Spirit catalog! (I am a ❏ counselor ❏ educator ❏ other)

name (please print) _____

street _____

city/state/zip _____

email _____

Visit *www.freespirit.com* to download excerpts, quizzes, and more!

Want to know more about *successful strategies* to meet the social, emotional, and educational needs of *every student*?

Free Spirit can help! We're the home of SELF-HELP FOR KIDS®, SELF-HELP FOR TEENS®, and other award-winning materials used by educators, counselors, and parents. Our practical, ready-to-implement strategies help adults make a positive difference in the lives of children. Mail this card for a FREE catalog. (And have one sent to a friend or colleague!)

Send me a Free Spirit catalog! (I am a ❏ counselor ❏ educator ❏ other)

name (please print) _____

street _____

city/state/zip _____

email _____

and send one to: (He/She is a ❏ counselor ❏ educator ❏ parent ❏ other)

name (please print) _____

street _____

city/state/zip _____

email _____

Visit *www.freespirit.com* to download excerpts, quizzes, and more!

free spirit
PUBLiSHiNG®

**Helping kids
help themselves™
since 1983**

www.freespirit.com

**Help kids build
themselves up—
from the inside out!**

BUSINESS REPLY MAIL
FIRST-CLASS MAIL   PERMIT NO. 26589   MINNEAPOLIS MN

POSTAGE WILL BE PAID BY ADDRESSEE

free spirit PUBLiSHiNG®

Department 843
217 Fifth Avenue North, Suite 200
Minneapolis, MN 55401-9776

Free Spirit Publishing
**Celebrating over 20 years
of reaching and teaching
children and teens.**

BUSINESS REPLY MAIL
FIRST-CLASS MAIL   PERMIT NO. 26589   MINNEAPOLIS MN

POSTAGE WILL BE PAID BY ADDRESSEE

free spirit PUBLiSHiNG®

Department 843
217 Fifth Avenue North, Suite 200
Minneapolis, MN 55401-9776

Additional Activities (Instructions for Students)

De-escalating Conflicts. Pair off with another student. Discuss a conflict that escalated either into a huge argument or a physical fight. Then picture using reflective listening, "Stop, Breathe, Chill," and other strategies you've learned to turn the conflict around. Then, with your partner, write a dialogue like the ones in *The Kids' Guide* to show what each person says and how the conflict gets worked out. Share your dialogue with the larger group.

Sparking a Turnaround. Make a promise to yourself that the next time you have a conflict, you will use your power to spark a turnaround. Get into the balcony by using "Stop, Breathe, Chill" and reflective listening. Be prepared to share with the group what happened.

SESSION 10
Using I-Messages

(pages 50–56 in *The Kids' Guide to Working Out Conflicts*)

Students will

- be introduced to the Win/Win Guidelines
- understand and practice using I-messages

Materials

- chart paper and markers
- "The Win/Win Guidelines and Rules for Using the Win/Win Guidelines" handout (page 43), two per student
- "Turnaround Point" and "To Spark a Turnaround" signs from Session 9

Preparation

- Make copies of "The Win/Win Guidelines and Rules for Using the Win/Win Guidelines" handout for each student.

- Write the following on chart paper:

The Win/Win Guidelines
1. Cool off.
2. Talk the problem over using I-messages.
3. Listen while the other person speaks, and say back what you heard.
4. Take responsibility for your part in the conflict.
5. Brainstorm solutions and choose one that's fair to both of you.
6. Affirm, forgive, thank, or apologize to each other.

Rules for Using the Win/Win Guidelines
- Tell the truth.
- Be respectful.
- Attack the problem, not the person.
- No blaming, no name-calling, and no negative face or body language.
- Work together toward a fair solution.

1. Checking In (10 minutes)

Briefly discuss what students have been doing at home or with friends and classmates to prevent conflict. Then ask: **How has good listening helped you prevent or deal with conflicts?** Point out and discuss how strategies like "Stop, Breathe, Chill" and good listening give people the power to spark a turnaround—to shift from escalating a conflict to resolving it. Use an example students provide in your discussion to highlight the turnaround point in a conflict and what the student did or could have done to spark a turnaround.

Ask: **What questions do you have about what you've been reading in *The Kids' Guide?***

2. Introducing the Win/Win Guidelines
(30 minutes)

Refer to the guidelines and rules you wrote on the chart paper. Read or have students read each guideline aloud. Explain that you will be working with the guidelines in order.

Discuss Guideline 1 briefly. Ask: **What are some safe, healthy things you can do to cool off or calm down when you're feeling stressed or angry?** Invite students to share their ideas. (For additional suggestions, see pages 73–74 of *The Kids' Guide.*)

Introduce and practice I-messages. Focus attention on Guideline 2. Explain that I-messages are a helpful skill for turning around conflicts and staying respectful.

Choose a student to help you show the difference between a you-message and an I-message. Face the student and say: **"You didn't return my book on time. You're so inconsiderate!"** Ask the student how it felt to be spoken to in this way.

Repeat the scene, this time using an I-message and speaking respectfully to the student: **"I'm annoyed to get the book back so late. I needed to return it to the library."** Ask the student if it felt different to be spoken to in this way. Why or why not?

Explain to the group that the second time you spoke you used an I-message. Refer to pages 52–56 in *The Kids' Guide.* Point out these key features of an I-message:

- It uses the word *I.*

- It tells how you feel, why you feel that way, and what you want or need.

- It doesn't accuse or blame the other person.

Ask students: **What are some other I-messages I could have used?** (*Examples:* "I'm annoyed because the book wasn't returned to me on time. Now it's overdue," or "I feel irritated because you didn't return my book on time.")

Note: The word *you* can be included in the I-message as long as it's not used in an accusatory or sarcastic way. *For example,* "I was upset when you didn't invite me to the party" is respectful and still focuses on how the speaker feels. Remind students to be aware of their tone of voice and body language when using I-messages. Any hint of blame or sarcasm will cancel out the positive value.

Have students pair up to do the "Try It" exercise on page 55 in *The Kids' Guide.* Circulate around the room and give help with I-messages as needed. Debrief afterwards so students can share their reactions. Let them know that using I-messages can feel awkward at first, but that it becomes more natural with practice.

Put the first two guidelines together. If time permits, ask students for an example of a real conflict—one that escalated and was not successfully resolved. Ask for two volunteers to act it out. Then ask for volunteers to replay the conflict, this time cooling off before they talk and using I-messages to begin talking about the problem. See if the conflict turns around. If it doesn't, ask the group to determine why, using questions like these:

- **Were either (or both) of the people too angry? Did they need to cool off more before talking? How could they have done that?**

- **Did anyone use you-messages? What happened?**

- **Did anyone use I-messages? How did I-messages help?**

- **What else might have turned the conflict around?**

3. Wrap-Up (5 minutes)

Give each student two copies of "The Win/Win Guidelines and Rules for Using the Win/Win Guidelines" handout. Have them staple or tape one copy in their notebooks and post the other copy at home. Encourage students to cool off and use I-messages when conflicts arise in the coming days.

If time permits, discuss ways students can use the guidelines at home. Suggest that students show and explain "The Win/Win Guidelines" to family members, talk about ideas for cooling off, and teach the difference between I-messages and you-messages.

End with a slogan, song, quote, or rap the students have made up.

4. Looking Ahead

• Assign the reading for Session 11: pages 57–60 in *The Kids' Guide*.

• Suggest that students choose three favorite cooling-off strategies for school and three for home and write them on the inside-front cover of their notebooks for easy reference.

• Remind students to bring completed "Conflict Logs" to the next session.

The Win/Win Guidelines

1. Cool off.

2. Talk the problem over using I-messages.

3. Listen while the other person speaks, and say back what you heard.

4. Take responsibility for your part in the conflict.

5. Brainstorm solutions and choose one that's fair to both of you.

6. Affirm, forgive, thank, or apologize to each other.

Rules for Using the Win/Win Guidelines

• Tell the truth.

• Be respectful.

• Attack the problem, not the person.

• No blaming, no name-calling, and no negative face or body language.

• Work together toward a fair solution.

The Win/Win Guidelines:
Taking Responsibility to Help Resolve Conflicts

(pages 57–60 in *The Kids' Guide to Working Out Conflicts*)

Students will

- understand how taking responsibility helps resolve conflicts
- understand where they are responsible in conflict situations
- begin to take responsibility for their role in conflicts

Materials

- completed "Conflict Logs" from previous sessions
- "Turnaround Point" and "To Spark a Turnaround" signs from Session 9
- "Taking Responsibility" handout (page 46), one per student

Preparation

- Make copies of the "Taking Responsibility" handout for each student.

1. Checking In (10 minutes)

Check in with students on how they used cooling off and I-messages since the last session. Were they able to work out conflicts more peacefully? Also, check in with them on whether they used the Win/Win Guidelines at home: **How did your family members react? Did the guidelines** help you work out conflicts at home? Why or why not?

2. Taking Responsibility for Your Role in Conflicts (30 minutes)

Have students turn to pages 57–58 in *The Kids' Guide.* Ask a student to read aloud the paragraph under "Take responsibility for your part in the conflict." Talk about it together, particularly the part about blaming. Ask: **Why is taking responsibility hard? Why does it take courage?**

Then ask students to look through their "Conflict Logs" and choose an unresolved conflict that they'd like to act out. Ask for a volunteer to act out the conflict, but instead of playing herself or himself, the volunteer should play the person with whom the conflict was. Have a second volunteer play the part of the first student. (You'll need to huddle for a few moments with the role players to explain this.)

After the role play, have the first student describe what it was like to play the role of the person the conflict was with, asking questions like:

• **Did you have a new understanding of the other person's point of view? Did you understand that person's behavior a little better?**

• **Did playing the other person help you see where you were responsible for how the conflict started or for how it turned out? Why or why not?**

Ask the second volunteer:

• **Did you feel the other person was taking responsibility?**

• **If the other person had taken more responsibility, how would it have affected your reaction? Would the conflict have been handled better?**

Now ask the whole group to evaluate the role play, focusing on the issue of responsibility: **How could**

taking responsibility have helped prevent or settle this conflict? Were both people responsible in some way? Or was one person more responsible? How?

Conduct a second role play with new students, using the same method. This time both students, but especially the person who escalated the conflict, should take responsibility for solving it. After the role play, discuss it with the group, asking questions like:

• **Did this conflict turn around? If so, how?**

• **How did taking responsibility help spark a turnaround?**

• **If the conflict didn't turn around, what went wrong?**

• **Would taking responsibility have helped?**

• **Do you think you'll be able to take responsibility the next time you have a conflict? Why or why not?**

3. Wrap-Up (5 minutes)

End with a slogan, song, quote, or rap students have come up with.

4. Looking Ahead

• Assign the reading for Session 12: pages 60–65 in *The Kids' Guide*.

• Ask students to complete the "Taking Responsibility" handout.

Taking Responsibility

Go through the conflicts in your "Conflict Logs." Choose one that was not resolved in a positive way. Answer the questions below:

Describe the conflict in a couple of sentences: _____

_____

_____

_____

_____

How was I responsible? _____

_____

_____

_____

_____

What could I have done to spark a turnaround? _____

_____

_____

_____

_____

Final questions

Why is it sometimes hard to take responsibility? _____

_____

_____

_____

_____

What is the benefit of doing so? _____

_____

_____

_____

_____

Would I be more willing to take responsibility the next time? If so, how? If not, why not? _____

_____

_____

_____

_____

The Win/Win Guidelines: Brainstorming Solutions and Affirming the Other Person

(pages 60–65 in *The Kids' Guide to Working Out Conflicts*)

Students will

- understand that there are many solutions to each conflict
- learn to brainstorm solutions to conflicts
- understand the importance of affirming the person they had the conflict with

Materials

- chart paper and markers
- completed "Taking Responsibility" handouts from Session 11

- completed "Conflict Logs" from previous sessions
- copies of "Using Brain Power to Find Solutions" handout (page 49), one per student

Preparation

- Make copies of "Using Brain Power to Find Solutions" handout for each student.

1. Checking In (10 minutes)

Have students take out their "Taking Responsibility" handouts from Session 11. Lead a discussion of what they learned by asking questions like:

- **How were you responsible for the conflict?**

- **Were you able to admit that you were responsible? Why or why not?**

- **If you had taken responsibility, how might that have sparked a turnaround in any of the conflicts?**

- **Do you think you'll be more able to take responsibility in the future? Why or why not?**

2. Brainstorming Solutions (25 minutes)

Have students refer to pages 61–62 in *The Kids' Guide*. Ask for volunteers to read aloud the dialogue between Joanie and Steph. (Or, if you prefer, have two students role-play it in front of the group.)

Ask the group to come up with all the things Steph did to help Joanie think twice about smoking cigarettes. List the students' ideas on chart paper. They will include:

• Gave Joanie good reasons not to smoke (*for example,* they are athletes).

• Reassured Joanie of her friendship.

• Told Joanie she cared.

• Gave an example of someone who was harmed by smoking.

• Told Joanie that smoking would come between their friendship.

• Looked for ways to compromise.

• Offered alternative ways to get out of the situation.

Next ask students to pair off. Distribute the "Using Brain Power to Find Solutions" handout and have students complete the handout in pairs.

Lead a discussion by asking questions like:

• **What happened in a recent conflict you had?**

• **How were you responsible for the conflict?**

• **What would you do differently the next time?**

• **If a good friend had the same conflict, what would you suggest your friend do?**

3. Wrap-Up (10 minutes)

Lead a discussion of the importance of affirming the person you have a conflict with. Ask the group what Joanie says to Steph at the end of their conversation. Ask students about real-life conflicts they've had: **Are you able to affirm, forgive, thank, or apologize to the people you have conflicts with? Why or why not?**

4. Looking Ahead

• Assign the reading for Session 13: pages 65–67 of *The Kids' Guide*.

Using Brain Power
to Find Solutions

Choose a conflict you had (recent or old) that didn't get worked out in a positive way. Then answer the following questions:

How was I responsible for the outcome? _____

_____

_____

If I had the same conflict again, what could I do differently? _____

_____

_____

If a good friend had the same conflict, what solutions would I suggest? Brainstorm five solutions that would be fair to both people:

1. _____

_____

2. _____

_____

3. _____

_____

4. _____

_____

5. _____

_____

Close your eyes, breathe deep. Think of something that makes you happy. When you open your eyes, see if you can think of five more solutions to the same conflict. It's okay to ask someone else for ideas if you get stuck:

1. _____

_____

2. _____

_____

3. _____

_____

4. _____

_____

5. _____

Applying the Win/Win Guidelines to Real-Life Conflicts

(pages 65–67 in *The Kids' Guide to Working Out Conflicts*)

Students will

- review the Win/Win Guidelines
- apply the Win/Win Guidelines to real-life conflicts
- learn how body language and nonverbal message contribute to conflicts

Materials

- chart paper and markers
- completed "Using Brain Power to Find Solutions" handouts from Session 12
- "Conflict Resolution Observation Sheet" handout (page 52), one per student

Preparation

- Make copies of the "Conflict Resolution Observation Sheet" handout.

1. Checking In (5 minutes)

Ask students about their reactions to the assigned reading. Also, ask about their reactions to conflict. What ideas are they putting into action and what has been the result?

2. Applying the Win/Win Guidelines to Real-Life Conflicts (30 minutes)

Ask students to suggest real-life conflicts they would like to act out. Choose one that the group

can relate to. Have the student who suggested it describe the conflict in detail and give some background on what led up to the conflict. *For example, is it ongoing? Are the kids friends? Are they in competing groups?*

Ask the student who suggested the conflict to play the part of his or her opponent. Ask for a volunteer to play the other part.

Before beginning the role play, write the Win/Win Guidelines and the Rules for Using the Win/Win Guidelines (see page 40) on chart paper. Ask a student to lead the group in reviewing the rules. Have the student ask the role players if they are willing to abide by these rules.

Then ask another student to lead the group in reviewing the Win/Win Guidelines. Remind the actors to keep an eye on the guidelines as they role-play so they'll be sure to cover each step. Let them know that this is important for practicing, but in real life they may not have to use every step every time.

Pass out the "Conflict Resolution Observation Sheet" handout. Make sure everyone understands each question. Direct the students to observe carefully and to take notes as they watch the role play. (If you would prefer not to use the sheets, simply have the students observe the role play and focus on the rules and guidelines as they watch. Or, assign students to watch for particular guidelines and rules.)

Conduct the role play. If either actor breaks one of the rules of the Win/Win Guidelines, stop the action and have the group remind the actors of what they need to do. (*For example,* any hostility is usually a sign that more cooling off time is needed.)

Debrief by having the group share what they observed, referring to their completed "Conflict Resolution Observation Sheets." Discuss the students' observations in detail. If there is time, conduct a second role play.

3. Wrap-Up (5 minutes)

End with a slogan, song, quote, or rap the students have put together.

4. Looking Ahead

- Assign the reading for Session 14: pages 68–74 of *The Kids' Guide.*

- Ask the students to use the Win/Win Guidelines with people in their lives. They should write in their notebooks about how this process went: **Were you able to resolve the conflict successfully? If so, what guidelines helped you? Were you responsible in some way for the conflict escalating? What guidelines did you fail to follow?**

Additional Activities (Instructions for Students)

"Yes, But" Questions. Take a look at the "'Yes, But' Questions" on pages 65–67 of *The Kids' Guide.* Can you relate to these questions? Do you have any "Yes, But" Questions of your own?

Win/Win Business Cards. Create a "business" card with the Win/Win Guidelines on one side and the Rules for Using the Win/Win Guidelines on the other. Carry it around with you for handy reference.

Conflict Resolution
Observation Sheet

During the role play, answer the following questions:

Are the role players sticking to the Rules for Using the Win/Win Guidelines? If not, which rules are they forgetting? _____

_____

_____

_____

Did the role players cool off enough before starting? Why or why not? _____

_____

_____

Are the role players using body language and facial expressions that will help solve the conflict peacefully? Why or why not? _____

_____

_____

Are the role players using a tone of voice that will help solve the conflict peacefully? Why or why not?

_____

_____

_____

Are both people taking responsibility for their role in the conflict? If not, why not? If so, how can you tell?

_____

_____

_____

Was the conflict resolved successfully? If not, what went wrong? _____

_____

_____

_____

If the conflict was resolved successfully, what did the people do to make it happen? _____

_____

_____

_____

Do you have any advice for either of the people involved in the conflict? _____

_____

_____

_____

_____

SESSION 14

Understanding and Gaining Control of Your Anger

(pages 68–74 in *The Kids' Guide to Working Out Conflicts*)

Note: A few students will need to design and illustrate a "Stop, Breathe, Chill" sign and a handout a few days in advance of this session.

Students will

• learn about their physical reactions to anger
• learn about how thoughts contribute to anger
• use a visualization activity to calm themselves

Materials

• "Managing Anger" handout (page 55), one per student

• chart paper and markers
• blank 8½" x 11" sheet of paper

Preparation

• A day or two before this session, ask a few students to design and illustrate a large "Stop, Breathe, Chill" sign and to create a matching 8½" x 11" handout. Make copies of the handout for each student.
• Make copies of the "Managing Anger" handout for each student.

1. Checking In (15 minutes)

Discuss how anger and the inability to manage it affects conflict—when we're angry, we tend to react rather than choose our responses, which can make things worse. Tell students there are ways to get a handle on how anger affects us. Say: **We can manage anger instead of letting anger manage us. But first we have to know more about how we react when we get angry before we can manage it.**

Pass out the "Managing Anger" handout. Have students work in pairs to fill it out and discuss the

anger issues that are most challenging to them. Ask the pairs to share their issues with the group.

2. Managing Anger (15 minutes)

Review the *fight-or-flight mechanism* (pages 69–70 of *The Kids' Guide*). Ask students: **What physical sensations do you feel when you're angry?** (*For example,* pounding heart, heat in the face, knot in the stomach, shakiness, sweating, and tension in the neck, jaw, or shoulders.) List these on the chart paper.

Now discuss how anger is also fueled by the thoughts we think. Ask students questions like:

- **What thoughts come into your head when you get mad?**

- **Do you think these kinds of thoughts make the anger worse?**

- **What can you do to calm those thoughts? (Review how calming statements can reduce the anger and give us more control.)**

- **What calming statements did you come up with in earlier sessions?**

- **Have you been using the calming statements when you get mad?**

- **Have your calming statements helped? Why or why not?**

Ask students to come up with two more calming statements. Have them write the statements in their notebooks and share them with the group. Let students know that they have the power to change their reactions to anger by using calming statements and "Stop, Breathe, Chill." There's also a new process they can learn called *visualization.*

3. "Stop, Breathe, Chill" Visualization
(10 minutes)

Display the "Stop, Breathe, Chill" sign and distribute the "Stop, Breathe, Chill" handouts to students. Practice the breathing, reminding students to inhale all the way down into the lower abdomen.

Ask students to close their eyes. (Kids who are uncomfortable doing this can cover the eyes or look down.) Say: **Bring into your mind a conflict you had, one where you felt very angry. Watch the conflict as though it were taking place now. Let yourself feel the anger.** Give students a few moments to envision this.

Say: **Now, erase the conflict from your mind and in its place picture a blank blue screen. Imagine yourself walking onto the screen feeling calm, relaxed, happy, and in complete control of yourself. Take some slow, deep abdominal breaths, and let each breath calm your mind and body**
even more. **Now bring the person you had the conflict with onto the screen. Imagine that the conflict is starting again. Picture yourself doing "Stop, Breathe, Chill." Take another slow deep breath as you picture yourself doing this. Repeat your calming statement in your head. Picture yourself getting a drink of water or doing something else to help you cool off. Now imagine yourself calm enough to resolve the conflict. See that happening now. Think of the words that are being spoken. Watch the conflict work out successfully. When you're finished, open your eyes.**

4. Wrap-Up (5 minutes)

Discuss the visualization with the group: **How did you feel during the exercise? How did the conflict turn out differently? Did doing this exercise give you a different view of how you react to conflicts? Do you think you could use this technique to calm yourself when conflicts are happening? Why or why not? Could you use the technique at other times?**

Point out to students that visualizing a technique often makes it easier to do the technique in real life.

5. Looking Ahead

- Suggest that students repeat the "Stop, Breathe, Chill" visualization before going to sleep at night or whenever they have an unresolved conflict. Let them know that practicing the visualization will help prepare them to face real conflicts calmly.

- Assign the reading for Session 15: pages 75–80 in *The Kids' Guide.*

Additional Activity (Instructions for Students)

Win/Win Dialogues. Write a dialogue between two people having a conflict. Write a second dialogue to show how the conflict gets resolved using "Stop, Breathe, Chill" and the Win/Win Guidelines. Act out your dialogue with someone else and videotape it to share with the group.

Managing Anger

Answer yes or no to the following statements.

When I'm angry with someone, this often happens . . .

_____ I lose my ability to think straight.

_____ I say or do something I regret later.

_____ I push, hit, punch, or kick.

_____ I curse or yell.

_____ I call the person names, give nasty looks, or use some other kind of put-down.

_____ I walk away and gossip about the other person.

_____ I say or do nothing right then, but afterwards get even.

_____ I sulk or feel crummy inside.

_____ I stuff my feelings down and try to ignore them.

_____ I take my feelings out on someone else.

_____ I decide the other person is an idiot.

What kind of results do you get when you do these kinds of things? What can you do differently?

SESSION 15

Becoming Zinger-Proof

(pages 75–80 in *The Kids' Guide to Working Out Conflicts*)

Students will

- understand how zingers lead to conflict
- create a personal insurance policy against zingers
- become more zinger-proof

Materials

- blank business cards or poster board
- cooling-off strategies in notebooks, from Session 10

Preparation

- Have one blank business card for each student, or cut up poster board into pieces the size of business cards.

1. Checking In (5 minutes)

Ask if students tried the "Stop, Breathe, Chill" visualization before going to sleep at night: **Were you able to picture yourself calming down? Could you envision a different outcome to conflicts you had? Does doing this exercise help you feel more calm and more confident about working out conflicts? Why or why not?**

2. Make Yourself Zinger-Proof (30 minutes)

Ask a student to read aloud the paragraph at the top of page 78 in *The Kids' Guide*: "The kids in my class are constantly using zingers...." Open a discussion about zingers by asking questions like:

- **What's a zinger?**

- **What kinds of zingers do kids use on each other?**

- **How do you feel when zingers are flying toward you? Toward other kids?**

- **How do zingers lead to conflict? Why does this happen?**

- **How do you respond when you're on the receiving end?**

- **How do you respond when other kids are being called names?**

- **How many of you like to throw zingers at other people? Why?**

- **How do you suppose the person receiving zingers feels?**

- **Does anyone feel like Abby (in the paragraph you just read)—unaffected by zingers? What helps you feel that way?**

Tell students that it's possible to strengthen yourself on the inside so the zingers can have little or no affect on you. Have students take a look at the "Write About It" on page 78 of *The Kids' Guide*.

Ask students to make three lists for creating a personal insurance policy against being affected by zingers:

List 1: all the things you're good at

List 2: all the people in your life who care about you, adults as well as kids

List 3: happy memories from as far back as you can remember to the present

Circulate among the students and give coaching as needed. Ask a few volunteers to share what they've written. One person's list may spark ideas in others, particularly students who have trouble coming up with the lists. Encourage students to add to their lists.

Have a student read aloud the last paragraph in the "Write About It" on page 78 of *The Kids' Guide*. Ask for students' reactions to this statement. Ask what else they can do if someone's zingers make them angry. Refer them to the cooling-off strategies they wrote in their notebooks during Session 10.

Ask students to come up with specific things that can help them be unaffected by zingers. Their list might include:

- calming statements

- deep breathing

- thinking about something on their personal insurance policy list

- deciding not to take it personally

- reminding themselves that this moment will pass

- walking away with their head held high

Distribute the business cards to students. Ask them to write one or two calming statements on their cards. Tell them to carry the cards with them and to refer to them whenever they have a conflict.

3. Practicing Being Zinger-Proof
(15 minutes)

Conduct a brief role play in which the first student uses zingers and the second student uses techniques—including items from her personal insurance policy—to avoid getting hooked. Repeat a second role play, if there is time.

End with a slogan, song, quote, or rap the students have come up with.

4. Looking Ahead

- Assign the reading for Session 16: pages 80–83 in *The Kids' Guide*.

- In their notebooks, ask students to list several people they can talk to if they are angry or upset, or need good advice on any matter. The list can include adults and kids at school, at home, in the neighborhood, or at a place of worship, or relatives and friends they can reach by phone or email.

SESSION 16
Using Visualization to Stay Cool

(pages 80–83 in *The Kids' Guide to Working Out Conflicts*)

Students will
• learn two visualization activities to stay cool and manage anger

Materials
• chart paper and markers

Preparation
• Review the Peace Shield and Light Shield visualizations you will be reading aloud to students for this session.

1. Checking In (5 minutes)

Remind students of and discuss with them the purpose of visualization or picturing things in their minds—that if they picture themselves doing something, it can help them do the techniques in real life.

2. Peace Shield and Light Shield Visualizations (30 minutes)

Tell students that today they'll be working on a powerful visualization technique that helps people feel safe and protected in threatening circumstances. Say: **When we can keep calm, we have a greater chance of staying safe and not doing things that escalate conflicts. The Peace Shield visualization can help you do this.**

Conduct the Peace Shield visualization on page 80 of *The Kids' Guide*. Read the following text very slowly and pause for 5–10 seconds between each part:

• **Close your eyes and think of something that makes you feel happy and peaceful.**

• **Let the good feelings fill you up.**

- **Now picture an invisible shield of protection gathering around you, keeping the good feelings in. Choose a color for your peace shield. Imagine it keeping you calm and protecting you from all harm.**

- **Take a slow deep breath to "lock in" the power of your peace shield.**

- **Keep your eyes closed and focus on this image.**

Ask students to open their eyes. Ask students:

- **Were you able to picture the Peace Shield?**

- **How did it feel to be surrounded by it?**

Tell students that the next part of this exercise, the Light Shield visualization, will help them feel even stronger and safer. Have them close their eyes again. Read the following aloud and pause for 5–10 seconds between each part:

- **Imagine yourself safe behind your peace shield. Picture its color. Take a deep breath to "lock in" the power of your peace shield once again.**

- **Now bring into your mind an image of a person who has a lot of anger or meanness. As you picture this person, keep envisioning yourself safe behind your peace shield. See yourself completely protected.**

- **Now picture yourself sending out a beam of light to surround this person. Imagine this person being completely contained behind a shield of light created by the beam you just sent out.**

- **Breathe deeply and feel a sense of safety and distance from this person.**

- **Picture yourself standing tall and walking away. Picture the other person dissolving into the light shield you have created. Take one more deep breath as you picture this.**

Have students open their eyes. Ask them how the Peace Shield visualization felt compared with the Light Shield visualization.

3. Wrap-Up (5 minutes)

Ask students: **How can these visualization techniques help you stay out of fights?** Point out that these techniques help lower the surge of adrenaline that can cause us to react by fighting. **By lowering the adrenaline, we can feel less nervous and upset. We can make clearer decisions. We can choose what we say or do, rather than just react. These techniques can also help us feel brave and calm inside, even if the other person is angry.**

4. Looking Ahead

- Assign the reading for Session 17: pages 84–88 of *The Kids' Guide.*

Additional Activity (Instructions for Students)

"Staying Out of Fights" Interview. Talk to a person you know who is good at staying out of physical or verbal fights. Ask the person the following questions.

- What helps you stay out of fights?

- How do you keep yourself calm when someone else says or does things to make you mad?

- If someone tried to start a physical fight with you now, what would you do?

- What advice do you have about staying out of fights?

- What's the most important thing to remember?

Then answer this question yourself: What did you learn from this person that you can use in your own life?

SESSION 17
Coping with Stress

(pages 84–88 in *The Kids' Guide to Working Out Conflicts*)

Students will

• understand how stress fuels conflict
• learn how to deal with stress in positive ways

Materials

• bulletin board paper
• thick-point markers in the following colors: red, orange, black, blue, purple, green
• "When I'm Under Stress" handout (page 62), one per student

Preparation

• Make copies of the "When I'm Under Stress" handout for each student.
• You'll be creating a "Word Wall." For this purpose, get some large bulletin board paper (the kind that comes on a roll) in white, yellow, or any light color. You'll need one long piece of it, at least 4 to 8 feet, depending on the size of the group. Hang it on the wall for use during the session. Make sure all students will be able to reach it to write on it. Otherwise, leave it on the floor and hang it later. Divide the sheet in half. On one side write "Stressors." On the other side write "De-stressors."

1. Checking In (25 minutes)

Review with students that we are more prone to fighting when we are under stress. Write the word "stress" on chart paper. Ask students:

• **How do you define stress?**

• **How do you feel when you're stressed out?**

• **What kinds of things stress you out the most?**

• **Does being under stress make you more or less able to work out conflicts?**

• **Does stress cause you to react rather than choose a response?**

Tell students that during the next activities they'll discover how stress affects them and what they can do about it. Pass out the "When I'm Under

Stress" handout. Have students form pairs to fill out the handout and discuss them. Ask them to jot down notes as they share.

Then discuss the handout with the larger group. Ask students:

- **What are your reactions to stress?**

- **What helps you to relieve stress?**

2. Word Wall (10 minutes)

Pass out the markers. Direct students' attention to the large bulletin board paper and tell them they'll be making a Word Wall. On the "Stressors" side of the bulletin board paper, have them write down in black, red, or orange the things that stress them out. If something is a big stressor, they can make the word big. They can "squiggle" the letters of words to make them look stressful.

On the "De-stressors" side, have students write in blue, green, and purple the things that help them deal with stress (*for example*, exercise, drawing, deep breathing, talking to friends, and so forth). Students can add small illustrations and symbols to each side.

3. Wrap-Up (10 minutes)

Review what students wrote on the Word Wall. Ask: **How can the de-stressors help you stay out of fights?**

4. Looking Ahead

- Assign the reading for Session 18: pages 88–91 of *The Kids' Guide.*

- Ask students to try at least one de-stressor listed on the Word Wall before the next session.

 # When I'm Under Stress

Put a check mark next to the things that happen to you when you're stressed out.

When I'm stressed. . .

_____ Everything gets on my nerves.

_____ I feel anxious, worried, or jumpy.

_____ My thinking gets foggy.

_____ I start to get dizzy.

_____ My heart pounds.

_____ My head aches.

_____ I can't sleep even though I'm tired.

_____ I want to sleep all the time.

_____ My stomach hurts.

_____ My skin breaks out.

_____ My palms get sweaty.

_____ I feel angry all the time.

_____ I have a short temper.

_____ I get bad thoughts in my head that won't go away.

What can you do to relieve stress?

SESSION 18
Peaceful Place Visualization

(pages 88–91 in *The Kids' Guide to Working Out Conflicts*)

Students will

- discover more ways to de-stress
- learn how to use the Peaceful Place visualization technique
- understand that they possess the power to calm themselves

Materials

- Word Wall from Session 17
- chart paper and markers
- two 3" x 5" note cards for each student

Preparation

- Review the Peaceful Place visualization you will be reading aloud to the students for this session.

1. Checking In (5 minutes)

Discuss with students the de-stressors they tried from the Word Wall. Did they help? How?

2. Peaceful Place Visualization (35 minutes)

Ask students: **Have you noticed that it's easier to stay out of conflicts when you're feeling calm?** Tell them they'll be learning a powerful calming strategy today: the Peaceful Place visualization. (Write the words on chart paper.) Explain that this is a process they can use anytime they feel stressed, frightened, depressed, angry, or anxious (including before tests).

Refer to the Word Wall from Session 17. Let students know that the process they are about to learn will help them deal with the stressful things they included on the "Stressor" side. Say: **We can't always control the stresses around us, but we *can* control the way stress affects us. The activity you are about to do is a powerful way to achieve calmness inside, no matter what is going on *outside* of you.**

Ask each student to think about a place they've been where they felt happy, peaceful, relaxed, and safe. It can be a place close to home or far away. It can be from the students' past, like their grandmother's kitchen when they were little. Tell students what your own peaceful place is. Describe it in detail, including colors, sounds, scents, and happy memories associated with this place.

Have students pair up to describe their peaceful places to one another.

> **Note:** If a student has trouble thinking of a peaceful place, you can suggest a place of calmness and beauty in your area (a park, a playground, a lake). Some kids have several peaceful places and aren't sure which one to choose. If that's the case, suggest that they use the first one that comes to mind.

After the discussion in pairs, ask the students to share their peaceful places with the large group. **What does the place look, smell, or sound like? What feelings do you have when you're there?**

Tell students that they'll be returning to their peaceful places now—in their imaginations. Ask them to close (or cover) their eyes and take a deep abdominal breath. Do this with them.

As students keep their eyes closed, read the following words in a slow, calming, rhythmic voice. Pause briefly between sentences so students have the chance to picture what you are describing:

Breathe slowly and deeply, and as you do, imagine that your mind is a blank movie screen. Your screen is the color blue, a bright, soothing shade of blue, like the sky on a clear spring day. Allow this image to fill your mind completely. Now project onto your screen an image of your peaceful place, where you felt happy, relaxed, peaceful, and safe. Let this peaceful place completely fill the screen of your mind. Allow it to grow so large that the screen melts away and all that's left is the picture of your peaceful place.

Now, step into your peaceful place. Imagine being there right now. Look around and notice **the colors. Now listen to the sounds of your peaceful place. Breathe deeply and inhale the scent of your peaceful place. Allow it to fill your nose, chest, head, arms, and legs. Allow the good feelings you had when you were last here to completely fill your body and mind. Let the good feelings fill your heart and radiate out into every cell, the way rays of sun touch everything around them. If distracting thoughts come into your mind, put them on a cloud and let the cloud carry them away. Then gently bring your focus back to your peaceful place and let the good feelings you had when you were last there completely fill you up.** (Pause a little longer).

Now feel yourself at ease and filled with a sense of well-being, confidence, and peace. Notice your smile, the brightness of your eyes, your calm sense of happiness. Keep picturing yourself this way, and allow the good feelings to fill you up.

Pause and allow a few moments for students to picture their peaceful place in silence. Have students open their eyes and welcome them back. Ask them to describe the feelings they had when they were in their peaceful places, experiencing their calm, confident selves. Some students may have had difficulty imagining their peaceful place. If this was the case, remind them that the more they practice, the easier it will get. In time, it will start to come more naturally.

> **Note:** As a follow up or an alternative activity to the visualization, you can have students draw, paint, or use pastels to re-create their peaceful place. Students can post the artwork in their homes or in the classroom or meeting room. A second alternative is to have students write a short description of their peaceful place, which volunteers can share with the group.

3. Wrap-Up (5 minutes)

Direct students' attention to the Word Wall. Ask them how doing the Peaceful Place visualization could help them when they face stress and conflict. Remind students that they always have the power to create a peaceful place. Encourage them to use this process whenever they want to feel calm.

4. Looking Ahead

- Assign the reading for Session 19: pages 91–98 of *The Kids' Guide.*

- Pass out note cards, two to a student. Ask students to read the empowerment statements on page 91 of *The Kids' Guide* and come up with at least three empowerment statements of their own. Tell them to write the statements on the two note cards. They should post one in their room and tape the other inside their notebooks. Tell them to say their empowerment statements every night before they go to bed and every morning when they wake up.

- Ask students to repeat the Peaceful Place visualization before they go to sleep at night.

SESSION 19
The Secret of 5/25

(pages 91–98 in *The Kids' Guide to Working Out Conflicts*)

Students will

- learn how they can change habits through the secret of 5/25
- identify how they want to change their reactions to conflict
- apply the secret of 5/25 to changing their reaction to conflicts

Materials

- Word Wall from Session 18
- chart paper and markers

Preparation

- Make a sign (or have a student make one):

Peace Begins with You

1. Checking In (5 minutes)

Check in with students about doing the Peaceful Place visualization at home. How did it feel to do it? Were they able to re-create their peaceful places? Can they see practicing visualizations on a regular basis, whenever they feel stressed or are facing a conflict? Remind them that the more they repeat the process, the easier it will get.

2. The Secret of 5/25 (25 minutes)

Review with students the calming strategies they've learned. Ask: **How can being a more peaceful person affect the way you relate to people? How can it help when it comes to conflict?**

Turn to "Activate the Secret of 5/25" on pages 91–92 of *The Kids' Guide*. Ask student volunteers to read the section aloud. Ask for their reactions to what was read: **If you practice a new skill for 5 minutes a day for 25 days, it can become a life-changing habit, one that can help you for the long-term. Do you believe this is true? What kinds of things have you practiced for 5 minutes a day (or more) to become skilled at?** (*For example,* sports, reading, art, music, and so on.)

Have the students work in pairs or groups of three. Ask them to think of things they can practice 5 minutes a day, at home, in school, or with their friends to help them work out conflicts. After a few minutes, ask the smaller groups to share their responses with the larger group. Their lists should include the techniques they've learned so far, such as:

• good listening/reflective listening

• calming statements

• "Stop, Breathe, Chill"

• putting yourself in the other person's place

• using I-messages

• putting aside willingness blocks

• choosing rather than reacting

• walking away rather than arguing or fighting

Students' lists should also include new techniques or ideas from their personal lives. *For example,* some students may mention calming activities they find helpful such as exercise, reading, music or art, meditation, and writing. Encourage a wide range of responses from the group.

3. Wrap-Up (15 minutes)

Display the sign: "Peace Begins with You." Lead a discussion of their reactions, by asking questions like:

• **What does this statement mean to you?**

• **How do the calming activities we've learned relate to this statement?**

• **How can being a calm and peaceful person affect our school, our community, or the world at large?**

4. Looking Ahead

• Assign the reading for Session 20: pages 99–104 of *The Kids' Guide.*

• Have the students select one item from their lists of things they want to practice and make a pledge to practice it 5 minutes a day until the next session.

Additional Activity (Instructions for Students)

Finding a Mentor. Another way to help yourself cope with the stresses of life is to have a mentor—a trusted adult who you can talk to and spend time with. Would you like to have a mentor in your life? If so, talk to a counselor, teacher, or youth leader. See if there's someone who can make time for you once a week or so. Here's a place you can call or email for more information: Big Brothers Big Sisters Association: (215) 567-7000, *www.bbbsa.org.* (*Note:* Leaders can research other local ways to find mentors.)

SESSION 20
Dealing with Teasing

(pages 99–104 in *The Kids' Guide to Working Out Conflicts*)

Students will

- distinguish between bullying and teasing
- discuss teasing and bullying in their lives
- learn techniques for dealing with teasing

Materials

- "Peace Begins with You" sign from Session 19
- "Dignity Stance" sign from Session 6
- chart paper and markers

Preparation

- None.

1. Checking In (15 minutes)

Lead a discussion on teasing and bullying, referring students to their own experiences and asking questions like:

- **Can anyone define bullying?** (When someone bullies, they intend emotional or physical harm.)

- **What's the difference between teasing and bullying?** (Teasing is meant to be light and harmless, and if both people involved enjoy it,

it can be fun. When teasing is used to have power over others, though, it's no longer teasing—it's bullying.)

- **Can anyone give an example of teasing that is bullying? That isn't bullying?**

- **Besides aggressive teasing, how do people bully?** (This will help students focus on the fact that until physical violence comes into play, most bullying is verbal taunting that becomes more and more cruel.)

- How many of you feel teasing and bullying are a big problem? Why?

- What kinds of teasing and bullying go on in school? Away from school?

- Why do you think people do it?

- How do teasing and bullying affect you personally?

2. Dealing with Teasing (20 minutes)

Ask volunteers to read out loud the "Eight Ways to Stop Teasing" on pages 102–104 of *The Kids' Guide.* You may also choose to write them on chart paper:

1. Try not to let the teasing get the best of you.

2. Agree with the teaser.

3. Ask the person to stop.

4. Walk away.

5. Avoid showing hurt or anger.

6. Talk to someone who can help.

7. Rehearse what you'll say next time.

8. Stick up for others and ask them to stick up for you.

Ask for two volunteers to do a short role play in which the first student teases the second student. The second student should use one or more of the methods listed above. Remind students to also use "Stop, Breathe, Chill," the Dignity Stance, empowerment statements, and exit lines.

After the role play, ask the actors for their reactions. Did the student who did the teasing find it hard to continue being aggressive? How did the second student feel about using the methods? Which methods would work best in real life? Why? Then ask for the group's reaction.

Ask for two new volunteers to do a second role play, using another of the methods listed or one of their own. Discuss the role play with the group.

When the role plays are finished, ask students what agreements they can make as a group to curtail teasing. Here are some suggestions:

- Don't do it if it really bothers you or someone else.

- If you're teasing someone and he or she is getting annoyed, back off.

- If you like to tease a lot, ask yourself why.

3. Wrap-Up (10 minutes)

Ask students to do a quick brainstorming: **What would you like your school to do to reduce teasing?**

List suggestions on chart paper. Consider using the suggestions in projects outside of the classroom or meeting room. *For example,* the suggestions could be decorated with artwork and displayed on hallway bulletin boards. Or the students could use the suggestions to make presentations to other classes or groups. See Session 23 (pages 76–77) for more guidance on school-wide projects.

4. Looking Ahead

- Assign the reading for Session 21: pages 104–108 in *The Kids' Guide.*

SESSION 21

Standing Up for Someone Who Is Being Bullied

(pages 104–108 in *The Kids' Guide to Working Out Conflicts*)

Students will

- identify the three roles in bullying
- understand how the roles contribute to bullying
- learn to stand up for kids who are being bullied

Materials

- chart paper and markers
- "Are You Bullying or Harassing Anyone?" handout (page 73), one per student

Preparation

- Make copies of the "Are You Bullying or Harassing Anyone?" handout for each student.

1. Checking In (10 minutes)

Open a discussion of bullying by asking students to define it. (Remind them of what they learned in the previous session—bullying is when someone purposely and repeatedly causes emotional or physical harm to a person.) Remind them that bullying is a form of violence, even when it isn't done physically.

Ask students if they can name the three roles in bullying. (The person who does the bullying, the person who gets picked on, and the bystanders.) Write the three roles on chart paper. Ask students to define *bystander*. (The bystander sees the bullying taking place. Emphasize that bystanders play an extremely important role. Bystanders often remain silent, laugh, do something to encourage the bullying, or join in themselves.)

2. Standing Up for Someone Who Is Being Bullied (25 minutes)

Refer to the terms you wrote on the chart paper:

- The person who bullies.

- The person who is bullied.

- The bystanders.

Let students know that most of us experience all three roles at some point in our lives. Share your own story and describe the roles you've played. Be honest. This will help students be honest, too. Ask which roles students have experienced. Discuss this in depth.

> **Note:** Students may be reticent to disclose that they have bullied others. Don't push. Allow the discussion to unfold.

Ask students about bullying in their school: **Does it happen often? Over what kinds of issues? Why do so many kids look the other way when someone is being picked on? Have you ever stood up for someone who was being bullied? Why or why not?**

Turn to pages 104–105 in *The Kids' Guide*. Ask for volunteers to take turns reading aloud the statistics on bullying. Talk about them.

Write the word "advocate" on chart paper. Ask what it means (someone who stands up for herself or himself or another person). Ask what bystanders can do to be advocates for kids who are picked on. List the responses on chart paper under the heading, "Standing Up for Others." Be sure to include the following:

- Join with a friend to speak up to the person who is bullying.

- Join with a friend to support the person who's being picked on (like asking the person to hang out with you).

- Don't bully the person who is bullying. Be assertive but respectful.

- If you're helping, don't let yourself get drawn into the problem. Say what you need to say, then walk away with your head held high.

Have students form pairs to brainstorm statements kids can say to stand up for someone who's being bullied. Caution against using threats or sarcasm. Here are some suggestions:

- "Not cool."

- "Don't criticize her just 'cause she's not you."

- "If you have a problem with him, there's a better way to handle it."

Ask students to share their statements with the larger group. List them on chart paper.

Do a 60-second role play where one student bullies another, and a third student plays the role of advocate. Remind advocates to breathe deeply, use the Dignity Stance, and to avoid sarcasm or an aggressive body posture and tone of voice. If there is time, conduct a second role play.

Discuss the role plays, by asking questions like:

- **Do you think this approach would work in a real-life bullying situation? Why or why not?**

- **Would you stand up for someone in this way?**

- **What other things can you do to help someone being bullied?**

3. Wrap-Up (10 minutes)

Pass out the "Are You Bullying or Harassing Anyone?" handout to students. Have students fill out the self-test. Then lead a "Trading Places" writing activity. Ask students to think of someone they picked on, were mean to, or bullied (including people in their families). Read the following passage aloud, pausing between each sentence:

Think of the person you acted mean toward, picked on, or bullied. Close your eyes for a moment and picture this person. Think about the hurtful words you said. Now imagine yourself as this person. Feel how this person might be feeling. Think this person's thoughts.

Have students open their eyes and begin to write down the thoughts and feelings this person might have had. Tell them they will be completing this assignment for homework and discussing it during the next session.

4. Looking Ahead

• Assign the reading for Session 22: pages 108–117 of *The Kids' Guide.*

• Ask students to finish the "Trading Places" writing activity.

Additional Activity (Instructions for Students)

Creating an Anti-Bullying Program in Your School. Request a meeting with the principal, guidance counselor, and school psychologist. Talk with them about starting a school-wide anti-bullying program, if you don't already have one. If you do have one, is it working? How can it be improved? Make this part of a "Peaceful School Action Plan."

Are You Bullying
or Harassing Anyone?

Some people know they bully—others bully without realizing it. They may not understand how much pain their mean actions can cause. To find out if you do things that could be considered bullying or harassment, take this quick self-test:

Regularly or often . . .

_____ I try to make another person feel bad.

_____ I make fun of a particular person.

_____ I take part in lots of name-calling.

_____ I purposely leave people out.

_____ I cause physical pain to another person.

_____ I threaten someone.

_____ I try to make somebody feel like she or he isn't as good as I am.

_____ I send mean notes, emails, or instant messages about someone else.

_____ I spread rumors about another person.

_____ I try to get others to do any of these things.

What can you do to be part of the solution, not part of the problem?

SESSION 22
Responding to Being Bullied

(pages 108–117 in *The Kids' Guide to Working Out Conflicts*)

Students will

- develop greater empathy for kids who are bullied
- understand what they can do if they are being bullied
- practice strategies to deal with being bullied

Materials

- "Trading Places" writing assignments from Session 21
- chart paper and markers

Preparation

- None.

1. Checking In (10 minutes)

Ask for volunteers to read aloud the "Trading Places" essays the students wrote. Discuss as a group, by asking questions like:

- **What did you learn from this activity?**

- **Did it help you to understand how bullying affects others? In what ways?**

- **Are you now more willing to avoid picking on someone or to stand up for someone who is being picked on? Why or why not?**

2. Standing Up to Someone Who Bullies (25 minutes)

Ask students how bullying takes place in their school. Ask them to volunteer a few scenarios to role-play (caution them about using real names). Write a sentence or two on chart paper about each scenario. Ask for volunteers to act out the first scenario.

Now have the group brainstorm strategies for the person who is being picked on. List them on the chart paper. List exit lines that kids who are bullied can use (see page 111 of *The Kids' Guide*, under "Assertive words"). Here are a few more:

- "You're wasting your energy."

- "This is not worth my time."

- "I'm not interested."

Repeat the role play again, this time with the person who is being bullied using the strategies that were discussed.

Afterwards, debrief with the entire group, by asking the following questions.

Did the student who was being picked on:
- **use the Dignity Stance?**

- **take deep breaths to calm down?**

- **get away from the situation in a timely manner or stick around too long, and open himself or herself to more abuse?**

- **use an exit line?**

- **do anything that made her or him more vulnerable?**

- **exhibit strength and courage?**

Make sure that the students take note of whether the role player put all the strategies together.

> ***Note:*** Caution students about sticking around too long in a bullying situation. Remind them that the best thing to do is to get themselves away as quickly as possible. Say: **Even if the person who's bullying is still saying things, walk away with your head held high and act as if the words aren't affecting you. Don't give your power away by reacting.**

Repeat the same role play a third time, but this time have two additional students participate as advocates who intervene on behalf of the person who is being picked on. Discuss with the group:

Were the students effective as advocates? Why or why not? What could they do differently the next time?

3. Wrap-Up (10 minutes)

Review the role plays with students. Ask them to relate what they just saw to their own lives, especially in terms of any teasing or bullying they see happening in school, by asking such questions as:

- **Could you see yourself using some of these strategies to stand up for yourself? Why or why not?**

- **If so, why do you think the strategies would work for you?**

- **If not, why do you think the strategies wouldn't work?**

- **What other strategies would you use if you're teased or bullied?**

- **Did the role play make you more confident about standing up for someone who is being bullied? Why or why not?**

4. Looking Ahead

- Assign the reading for Session 23: pages 119–121 of *The Kids' Guide*.

- Let students know that you'd like them to come up with their own poems, songs, raps, skits, or essays on resolving conflict and standing up for others. Tell them to work on this for the next session. (You can plan to have them share this work with the group, or compile it in a book, post it on bulletin boards in the building, or make presentations to other classes or groups, to parents, or in other forums. Another option is to present the group's work in a school-wide or organization-wide assembly, although this requires a great deal more planning.)

Spreading the Word About Working Out Conflicts

(pages 119–121 in *The Kids' Guide to Working Out Conflicts*)

Note: Many of the activities described below apply to school settings, but you will also find ideas that work in organizations and programs outside of school as well.

Students will

- discuss the importance of spreading the word about conflict resolution
- develop a plan for spreading the word in their school

Materials

- chart paper and markers

Preparation

- Will vary depending on the activity selected.

1. Checking In (10 minutes)

Discuss the importance of spreading the word about avoiding conflicts and working out conflicts peacefully. Why is it important? What should other kids know? What should adults know? What is the best way to get the message to them?

2. Discussing School-Wide Projects (25 minutes)

Have students break into groups to discuss the best ways to spread the word about conflict resolution. What were the most important lessons learned? What are the best ways of getting that message to other kids? Certainly writing and art-work are two ways of getting the message across. Students can write poems, essays, plays, skits, raps, songs, or other material that they can present to other classes or groups. Or they can use artwork alone or in combination with writing to spread the word. Encourage the groups to be creative in their thinking. Tell them that they know best what will reach their peers.

Here are other suggestions you can make for school-wide projects:

Teach the Win/Win Guidelines to Other Classes or Groups. Visit a class of younger kids. Share what you've been learning. Make them a copy of the Win/Win Guidelines to post in their class. Create a skit or role play to show them how to use the guidelines.

Introduce the Win/Win Guidelines to Your School. Plan an assembly where the group can introduce the Win/Win Guidelines to the whole school. Have students put together role plays and skits to perform at the assembly. Ask them to come up with a rap or song (or use the ones they've performed during the sessions) to teach to the whole school. Have students videotape their performance to share with family adults at a school function. Make copies of the video to share with other schools.

"Stay Out of Fights" Poster Campaign. Have students create posters that illustrate strategies for staying out of fights. They can hang the posters around the school. Have students take the posters to other classes or groups and talk about different strategies for staying out of fights.

Kids Mentor Kids to Stay Out of Fights. Buddy up with a younger grade class. Have students teach their younger buddies the strategies they are learning for staying out of fights.

Declare a "No Teasing Day" or Make a "No Fighting" Pledge. Have students take a pledge to refrain from teasing for a whole day. Or encourage them to start a "Safe Community/Safe School" campaign where kids take a "No Fighting" pledge.

Daily Messages. Brainstorm daily messages for the school. Have a group of students contact the principal about displaying these messages in and around the building and/or doing them as announcements.

Anti-Bullying Bulletin Board. Create a group bulletin board that displays some of the concepts the group has been learning. Have students include the statistics on bullying listed on pages 104–105 of *The Kids' Guide*.

Anonymous Essay Program for Anti-Bullying. Have students initiate a school-wide essay-writing program where kids can share their experiences of being bullied. Have the essays posted throughout the building. In one school, an anti-bullying movement was created as the result of similar essays. Teachers came onboard once they grasped the impact of bullying on their students' lives. Make it anonymous so kids won't be afraid to reveal their real experiences.

Peaceful Place Illustrations. Students can draw, paint, or use pastels to re-create their peaceful places. Display them in the school.

3. Wrap-Up (10 minutes)

Ask the smaller groups to share their ideas for school projects. List the ideas on chart paper. Get feedback from the group as a whole. Prioritize among the suggested projects, according to which are most realistic in terms of time, resources, and your particular setting. You will need to devote additional sessions to finalizing and planning the project, but this session has set the groundwork for proceeding.

4. Looking Ahead

- Assign the reading for Session 24: pages 121–126 of *The Kids' Guide*.

SESSION 24
The Power of Forgiveness

(pages 121–126 in *The Kids' Guide to Working Out Conflicts*)

Students will

- understand that forgiveness is an essential part of being peaceful
- understand that holding onto resentment prevents us from working out conflicts
- take steps toward forgiving someone who has hurt them

Materials

- chart paper and markers
- copies of the "Forgiveness Statement" handout (page 80), one per student (optional activity)

Preparation

- Makes copies of the "Forgiveness Statement" handout for each student.

1. Checking In (10 minutes)

Write the word "forgiveness" on chart paper. Ask students:

- **Why is forgiveness an essential element of peacemaking?**

- **Why is it sometimes hard to forgive someone who has hurt us?**

Tell students: **Forgiveness doesn't mean you have to accept what's unacceptable or act like it's okay. What it does mean is being willing to let go of the resentment you've been holding onto. It's saying to yourself, "I won't let this anger take up space in my brain anymore."** Discuss this concept.

2. The Power of Forgiveness (25 minutes)

Write the word "resentment" on chart paper. Ask what it means (holding onto angry feelings over time). Ask students:

• **How can resentment hurt us?** (It can make us anxious, depressed, even physically sick. It can lower our immune systems.)

Ask a student to read the Nelson Mandela quote on the bottom of page 121 of *The Kids' Guide:* "Holding onto resentment is like drinking poison and hoping it will kill your enemy." Explain who Nelson Mandela is—as a black South African, he was imprisoned for almost 30 years because he fought for equality for nonwhite South Africans. This was at a time when that country was run by white people under a social and legal system called *apartheid.* Under apartheid, white South Africans had the freedom to live, go to school, and work wherever they wanted, while people of color did not. When Mandela was finally released from jail, apartheid ended and he soon became president of South Africa.

Then ask the group:

• **What does Mandela's statement mean to you? Do you agree with him? Why or why not?** (Tell them that Mandela made the choice to forgive the people who had imprisoned him and led the country in helping others forgive as well. He did this so both he and the country could heal.)

Help students understand that holding onto resentment causes a chain reaction: we think of the person who harmed us, then we reopen the wound by replaying what happened. We end up hurting ourselves, not the person we resent.

Forgiveness is about saying, "I will no longer allow that person to have power over me in my thoughts. I'm moving on."

Tell students that forgiving also doesn't mean allowing the person to hurt you again. It's more about not hurting yourself by holding onto negative emotions.

Involve students in a more personal discussion of forgiveness, by asking questions like:

• **Have you ever been forgiven for something?**

• **Is there anyone in your life you haven't forgiven?** (Remind them that no one has to share personal information unless they feel comfortable doing so.)

• **If you were able to forgive this person, how could you do it?**

Ask for their suggestions, such as speaking to the person, writing the person a note, or offering to do something nice for that person. Ask if they would consider taking that next step. What stands in the way of taking that next step?

3. Wrap-Up (10 minutes)

End with a slogan, song, quote, or rap the students have selected.

Hand out copies of the "Forgiveness Statement" and ask students to fill it out at home if they wish. It is an optional activity for those students who wish to do it.

4. Looking Ahead

• Assign the reading for Session 25: pages 127–133 of *The Kids' Guide.*

Forgiveness Statement

If you have someone you need to forgive, fill out the following:

_____ is someone I've been holding onto resentment toward.

Here's why: _____

_____

_____

As the result of what happened I decided: _____

_____

_____

_____

When I see _____ here's what I usually do: _____

_____

_____

I am holding onto my anger because _____

_____

_____

Here's how I might feel if I decide to forgive: _____

_____

_____

Here's what I need to communicate so I can forgive: _____

_____

_____

_____

_____

Forgiving will help me let go of resentment and anger and feel more peaceful.

Now complete the following:

(This is just for you. You don't need to show it to anyone else unless you want to.)

> I _____ hereby grant forgiveness to _____
>
> for _____.
>
> **I am now making a conscious decision to let go of the anger I've been holding onto.**
>
> _____
>
> (sign your name here)

SESSION 25
Using a Day-by-Day Plan

(pages 127–133 in *The Kids' Guide to Working Out Conflicts*)

Students will

- review what they have learned about working out conflicts
- learn how to keep these lessons alive through a "Conflict Solver's Action Plan"
- continue being a part of the solution to conflict, violence, and bullying

Materials

- chart paper and markers
- "Conflict Solver's Action Plan" (Days 1–7) (pages 83–89), one each per student

Preparation

- Make copies of the "Conflict Solver's Action Plan" handouts for each student.

1. Checking In (15 minutes)

Ask students to orally list the most important things they learned from the sessions. List their answers on chart paper as they speak.

Acknowledge students for the progress they've made and ask if there's anyone in the room they would like to acknowledge (for kindness, good listening, being respectful, growth, or courage).

2. Conflict Solver's Action Plan (15 minutes)

Ask a student to read aloud the first paragraph on page 126 of *The Kids' Guide*. Talk about it together.

Ask students if doing conflict resolution has improved their lives. In what ways? Challenge them to continue making conflict resolution a lifelong habit.

Tell students that the "Conflict Solver's Action Plan" will help them continue putting the skills they've learned into practice.

Have students turn to pages 127–133 of *The Kids' Guide*. Together, go over each page. Have different students take turns reading pages or sections they choose.

Discuss the routine of waking up each morning and using a page a day from the "Conflict Solver's Action Plan" to help them stay on track. Suggest the following routine:

- **Put *The Kids' Guide* on your dresser before you go to bed.**

- **When you wake up in the morning, turn to the "Conflict Solver's Action Plan" first thing (or keep a copy of the plan near your bed).**

- **Repeat aloud the empowerment statement at the top of the page you're on.**

- **Read the action steps and choose at least one. Promise yourself to take that action throughout the day.**

- **Try writing down the action step on note paper and keep it with you as a reminder.**

- **At the end of the day, check in with yourself. Did you keep the promise you made to yourself in the morning? Acknowledge yourself if you did. If not, what would help for next time?**

Talk about what students have planned and what they've done. Compliment them for whatever they've accomplished. Encourage them to think long-term and keep adding to the plans they've made.

3. Wrap-Up (15 minutes)

Have students come up with individual promises regarding what they will do as peacemakers at school, at home, or in the community. Ask students to write down a peacemaking promise that they intend to keep.

Ask each student to share the promises she or he made. Acknowledge the work students have done and will continue to do to make their school, home, and community more peaceful.

4. Looking Ahead

- Ask students to start tomorrow morning with Day 1 of the "Conflict Solver's Action Plan." Tell them to continue with a new page on each following day. After Day 7, they should start over.

Day 1: Keep an open mind.

> ## Today's empowerment statement:
>
> I feel good on the inside when I choose
> the balcony over the basement.

Actions I can take today:

 I'll be willing to work out conflicts instead of fighting.

 I'll stop and take a deep breath whenever I get mad.

 I'll take responsibility for my role in conflicts.

 I'll be willing to take the first step to work out
a conflict.

 I'll resist the urge to blame.

Day 2: Choose to solve conflicts.

Today's empowerment statement:

My words and actions are respectful.

Actions I can take today:

 I'll use a calming statement when I feel upset, angry, or tense.

 I'll stand up for myself without going on the attack.

 I'll act brave, strong, and respectful even if my feelings pull me in another direction.

 I'll stay in the balcony even when others are in the basement.

Day 3: Become a better listener.

Today's empowerment statement:

Listening helps me get along better
with the people in my life.

Actions I can take today:

 I'll focus on the speaker.

 I'll resist the urge to interrupt or to let my mind
drift off when someone is speaking.

 I'll use reflective listening to understand another
person's feelings and point of view.

 I'll focus on listening if I'm in a conflict with
someone.

Day 4: Use Win/Win Guidelines.

> ## Today's empowerment statement:
>
> I can resolve conflicts peacefully.

Actions I can take today:

 I'll cool off so I can talk things over respectfully.

 I'll use I-messages to express my point of view.

 I'll compromise and seek solutions.

 I'll remember to attack the problem, not the person.

 I'll choose working it out over fighting it out.

Conflict Solver's Action Plan
Day 5: Manage anger.

> ### Today's empowerment statement:
> I have the power to control my anger.

Actions I can take today:

 If I feel angry I'll stop, breathe, and chill before reacting.

 I'll list things that can help me cool off and use them when I need them.

 I won't get hooked by zingers.

 I won't use put-downs.

 I'll seek an adult's help with anger if I need to.

 I'll show courage by walking away from fights with my head held high.

Day 6: Manage stress.

Today's empowerment statement:

I have what I need inside to keep cool and calm.

Actions I can take today:

 I'll start my day with deep breathing and visualize my confident self.

 I'll use my empowerment statement throughout the day.

 I'll de-stress in healthy ways.

 I'll spend time with someone who cares about me.

 I'll cut back on TV and video games.

 I'll end my day with a calming activity like deep breathing, yoga, or meditation.

Day 7: Be smart about bullying.

Today's empowerment statement:

I can be strong and kind at the same time.

Actions I can take today:

 I'll take responsibility and make amends if I have hurt anyone in the past.

 I'll stop myself immediately from hurting someone physically or with my words.

 I'll get help or act assertively if someone tries to bully me.

 I'll find an adult who can help me deal with problems I can't solve on my own.

 I'll stick up for someone who's being teased, picked on, put down, or bullied.

 I'll ask my friend to stick up for someone who's being bullied, too.

Supplemental Materials

What I've Learned
About Working Out Conflicts

Step 1: Open Your Mind (pages 1–18 in *The Kids' Guide to Working Out Conflicts*)

1. What are three positive choices for handling a conflict?

   • _____

   • _____

   • _____

2. What are three negative choices for handling a conflict?

   • _____

   • _____

   • _____

3. List three common conflict triggers.

   • _____

   • _____

   • _____

4. List three common willingness blocks that prevent people from solving conflicts.

   • _____

   • _____

   • _____

5. Write a one- or two-paragraph response to one of the following:
   • When faced with a conflict, what does it mean to choose between the basement and balcony?
   • How can a conflict inside your head escalate to a conflict with other people?
   • What happens when people are not willing to work out conflicts?
   • How can one person's bad mood lead to a fight or a conflict?

   _____

   _____

   _____

   _____

   _____

   _____

   _____

   _____

   _____

What I've Learned
About Working Out Conflicts

Step 2: Decide to Become a Conflict Solver (pages 20–34 in *The Kids' Guide to Working Out Conflicts*)

1. Describe a three-step technique that can help you stay calm in a conflict. How will this help you?

    *   _____
    *   _____
    *   _____

2. What are three things you can do when your friends have conflicts?

    *   _____
    *   _____
    *   _____

3. Write a one- or two-paragraph response to one of the following:

    *   How can you be a conflict solver when the other person isn't willing?
    *   What should you do when you've tried all of the conflict solver techniques but you still can't reach a resolution?

    _____
    _____
    _____
    _____
    _____
    _____
    _____
    _____
    _____
    _____
    _____
    _____
    _____
    _____
    _____
    _____
    _____
    _____
    _____

What I've Learned
About Working Out Conflicts

Step 3: Becoming a Better Listener (pages 37–49 in *The Kids' Guide to Working Out Conflicts*)

1. While in a conversation, what are three things you can do to show you're listening?

- _____
- _____
- _____

2. While in a conversation, what are three signs that show someone is *not* listening?

- _____
- _____
- _____

3. Write a one- or two-paragraph response to one of the following:
   - How does good listening put you on the path to personal power?
   - What is reflective listening? How can it prevent conflicts from escalating?

_____
_____
_____
_____
_____
_____
_____
_____
_____
_____
_____
_____
_____
_____
_____
_____
_____
_____
_____

What I've Learned
About Working Out Conflicts

Step 4: Use Win/Win Guidelines (pages 50–67 in *The Kids' Guide to Working Out Conflicts*)

1. What are three of the six Win/Win Guidelines?

- _____
- _____
- _____

2. What are I-messages? When confronted with a problem, how can using I-messages help? Give an example of an I-message. _____

_____

_____

_____

3. Write a one- or two-paragraph response to one of the following:

- If using I-messages doesn't work, what questions can you ask yourself to better understand the situation?
- Why is it important to take responsibility for your part in a conflict?

_____

_____

_____

_____

_____

_____

_____

_____

_____

_____

_____

_____

_____

_____

_____

_____

_____

_____

_____

What I've Learned
About Working Out Conflicts

Step 5: Manage Your Anger and Gain Control (pages 68–83 in *The Kids' Guide to Working Out Conflicts*)

1. What are four things you can do to avoid a fight if someone is trying to start one?

- _____
- _____
- _____
- _____

2. When using "Stop, Breathe, Chill" to manage your anger, what are three affirmative, calming statements you can say to yourself to gain control?

- _____
- _____
- _____

3. Write a one- or two-paragraph response to one of the following:

- What is a zinger? What does it mean to be zinger-proof?
- What is a Peace Shield? How can it help you control your anger?
- How does empathizing help solve conflicts?

_____
_____
_____
_____
_____
_____
_____
_____
_____
_____
_____
_____
_____
_____
_____

What I've Learned
About Working Out Conflicts

Step 6: Learn to Manage Stress and Stay Calm, Cool, and Confident (pages 84–98 in *The Kids' Guide to Working Out Conflicts*)

1. What is the secret of 5/25? _____

    _____

    _____

    _____

2. What are a few things people can do to help themselves stay calm under stress?

    • _____

    • _____

    • _____

    • _____

3. Write a one- or two-paragraph response to one of the following:

    • Why is managing stress and anger an important part of being a conflict solver?

    • What are empowerment statements? How can using them help manage stress?

    _____

    _____

    _____

    _____

    _____

    _____

    _____

    _____

    _____

    _____

    _____

    _____

    _____

    _____

    _____

    _____

    _____

    _____

What I've Learned
About Working Out Conflicts

Step 7: Be Smart About Bullying (pages 99–117 in *The Kids' Guide to Working Out Conflicts*)

1. What is bullying? _____

    _____

    _____

    _____

2. List four of the eight ways to stop teasing.

    *   _____

    *   _____

    *   _____

    *   _____

3. Write a one- or two-paragraph response to one of the following:

    *   Why do people bully?

    *   How can you stand up to someone who is bullying you?

    *   Why is it important to take a stand against bullying? How can this be done?

    _____

    _____

    _____

    _____

    _____

    _____

    _____

    _____

    _____

    _____

    _____

    _____

    _____

    _____

    _____

    _____

    _____

    _____

What I've Learned
About Working Out Conflicts

Step 8: Build Yourself Up from the Inside Out (pages 119–133 in *The Kids' Guide to Working Out Conflicts*)

1. Why does it take courage to become a conflict solver? _____

    _____

    _____

    _____

2. How will a day-by-day plan help you be an effective conflict solver? _____

    _____

    _____

    _____

3. Write a one- or two-paragraph response to one of the following:

    • How will you use what you've learned about working out conflicts to bring more peace to your relationships and your community?

    • What is the most surprising or helpful thing you've learned about working out conflicts? What did it teach you about yourself?

    _____

    _____

    _____

    _____

    _____

    _____

    _____

    _____

    _____

    _____

    _____

    _____

    _____

    _____

    _____

    _____

    _____

What I've Learned
About Working Out Conflicts

Final Summary Questions (*The Kids' Guide to Working Out Conflicts*, all chapters)

1. What is a conflict? _____

    _____

    _____

    _____

2. What choices do you have when it comes to conflict? _____

    _____

    _____

    _____

3. Describe five things you can do to be a good listener.

    - _____
    - _____
    - _____
    - _____
    - _____

4. Explain reflective listening and give an example. _____

    _____

    _____

    _____

5. What are the six guidelines for working with another person to resolve a conflict?

    - _____
    - _____
    - _____
    - _____
    - _____
    - _____

6. Explain I-messages and give an example. How can I-messages help during conflict? _____

    _____

    _____

    _____

    _____

more ⟶

7. Why is managing anger and stress an important part of being a conflict solver? _____

_____

_____

_____

8. Describe a three-step technique that can help you stay calm in a conflict. How will this help you?

_____

_____

_____

_____

9. What is bullying? _____

_____

_____

_____

10. Write one- or two-paragraph response to one of the following:
    - When faced with a conflict, what does it mean to choose between the basement and balcony?
    - Why is it important to take responsibility for your part in a conflict?
    - Why is it important to take a stand against bullying? How can this be done?
    - Why does it take courage to become a conflict solver?
    - How can you be a conflict solver when the other person isn't willing?

_____

_____

_____

_____

_____

_____

_____

_____

_____

_____

_____

_____

_____

_____

_____

_____

What I've Learned About Working Out Conflicts

Step 1: Open Your Mind

1. Cooling off; listening; talking things out; taking deep breaths.

2. Teasing; put-downs; name-calling; physical violence; bullying; sarcasm.

3. Who's right/wrong; bragging; name-calling/insults/teasing; gossip/rumors; feeling jealous/left out; sharing; chores; interrupting/ignoring; who started the fight; who gets to use the phone.

4. Want to be "right"; don't want to appear weak; don't like someone; don't want to look stupid; feeling too angry; don't know how to change approach to conflicts; want to get even.

5. Answers will vary.

Step 2: Decide to Become a Conflict Solver

1. "Stop, Breathe, Chill." Using this technique will help you choose how to respond rather than react emotionally.

2. Try not to take sides; don't get involved in gossip; put yourself in their place; suggest mediation.

3. Answers will vary.

Step 3: Becoming a Better Listener

1. Answers should relate to the following: make eye contact; don't interrupt; stay focused on the speaker; ask questions; act like the speaker is the only person in the room; lean in and nod to show that you're interested.

2. Answers should relate to the following: looking around the room, no direct eye contact; interrupting the speaker; changing the subject; acting disinterested; turning body away from the speaker; fidgeting; asking about things the person already said.

3. Answers will vary.

Step 4: Use Win/Win Guidelines

1. Cool off; talk the problem over using I-messages; listen while the other person speaks and say back what you heard; take responsibility for your part in the conflict; brainstorm solutions and choose one that's fair to both of you; affirm, forgive, thank, or apologize to each other.

2. I-messages use the word *I* and tell how you feel and what you need without blaming or accusing the other person. In a conflict, I-messages can help you talk to the other person respectfully and keep things from escalating. Examples will vary.

3. Answers will vary.

Step 5: Manage Your Anger and Gain Control

1. Answers should relate to the following: try talking respectfully; suggest a time-out; put yourself in the other person's place; play it safe if you're in danger; leave the scene and ask for help.

2. Answers should relate to the following: I can handle this; I can keep my cool; I am in control; I have the power to stay calm; no one can make me feel bad about myself; peace is inside me; I have the strength to stay out of fights.

3. Answers will vary.

Step 6: Learn to Manage Stress and Stay Calm, Cool, and Confident

1. If you practice a new skill or technique for 5 minutes a day for 25 days you'll turn something new into a life-changing habit.

2. Answers should relate to the following: Find a quiet spot to sit; meditate; get exercise; express yourself through art, music, or writing; spend time with someone who's close to you; take deep breaths.

3. Answers will vary.

Step 7: Be Smart About Bullying

1. Bullying is teasing or physical contact that is deliberately meant to be harmful. When a person or group of people repeatedly picks on others in order to have power, it's bullying.

2. Try not to let the teasing get the best of you; agree with the teaser; ask the person to stop; walk away; avoid showing hurt or anger; talk to someone who can help; rehearse what you'll say next time; stick up for others and ask them to stick up for you.

3. Answers will vary.

Step 8: Build Yourself Up from the Inside Out

1. Courage leads to confidence, which in turn leads to greater self-respect and self-esteem. In order to be an effective conflict solver it helps to feel good about yourself and to not be deterred by bullies or those who are unwilling to work out conflicts.

2. A day-by-day plan with empowerment statements and action plans will help you apply peaceful principles to your daily life and conflicts.

3. Answers will vary.

Summary Questions

1. A conflict is a misunderstanding, disagreement, or fight between two or more people. It can also be something that goes on inside yourself.

2. Answers may include: choosing balcony or basement; choosing to behave with dignity and respect rather than escalating the conflict; choosing to be willing to work with the other person.

3. Answers may include: keeping eye contact; showing interest by leaning in and nodding; focusing on what the speaker is saying; not interrupting; not being distracted; asking questions so you understand; using reflective listening.

4. With reflective listening you say back (reflect) what you heard the other person saying, not by repeating word for word but by paraphrasing (using different words). Examples of reflective listening statements will vary.

5. 1. Cool off.

    2. Talk the problem over using I-messages.

    3. Listen while the other person speaks, and say back what you heard.

    4. Take responsibility for your part in the conflict.

    5. Brainstorm solutions and choose one that's fair to both of you.

    6. Affirm, forgive, thank, or apologize to each other.

6. I-messages use the word *I* and tell how you feel and what you need without blaming or accusing the other person. Examples will vary. In a conflict, I-messages can help you talk to the other person respectfully and keep things from escalating.

7. Answers should include the idea that unmanaged anger and stress can lead you to say and do things you may regret and can escalate the conflict.

8. "Stop, Breathe, Chill." Using this technique will help you choose how to respond rather than react emotionally.

9. Answers should include the concept that someone who bullies intends to do emotional or physical harm.

10. Answers will vary.

Resources

Books

And Words Can Hurt Forever: How to Protect Adolescents from Bullying, Harassment, and Emotional Violence by James Garbarino, Ph.D., and Ellen Delara, Ph.D. (New York: Free Press, 2002). The authors compiled data from interviews with students, educators, and administrators to address violence and safety in American schools. With an emphasis on school management, topics range from emotional violence and stalking to coping with the pressure and exclusivity of social cliques. A valuable resource for a multi-faceted approach to improving conflict resolution practices within the school environment.

The Bully, the Bullied, and the Bystander by Barbara Coloroso (New York: First HarperResource/Quill, 2004). This book offers an analysis of the cycle of bullying and the suffering, silence, and sadness that adolescents endure. With clear, detailed scenarios, the author elucidates each role and phase in the cycle of bullying and suggests solutions for parents and educators to rid schools of this harmful epidemic.

The Bully Free Classroom by Allan L. Beane, Ph.D. (Minneapolis: Free Spirit Publishing, 1999). A developer of bully prevention programs across the nation, the author outlines clear intervention strategies to change bullying behavior and helpful information to arm students with the assertive language skills they need to protect themselves from bullying. Also includes discussion questions, activities, and 45 reproducible pages.

Bullying at School: What We Know and What We Can Do by Dan Olweus (Cambridge, MA: Blackwell Publishers, 1993). Based on a comprehensive, communal effort to end bullying, the author advises parents and educators on how to implement a "whole school approach" by giving readers the tools to recognize bullying behavior and those who are suffering.

Healthy Anger: How to Help Children and Teens Manage Their Anger by Bernard Golden, Ph.D. (New York: Oxford University Press, 2003). *Healthy Anger* helps parents and educators understand the frustration and anger their children experience. The author assures the reader that anger is natural and healthy and shows how it can be used as a tool to foster greater understanding and help build stronger, more loving relationships.

Hot Stones & Funny Bones: Teens Helping Teens Cope with Stress & Anger by Brian Luke Seaward and Linda Bartlett (Florida: HCI Books, 2002). An accessible guide to help teens understand and control their stress and anger through first-hand narratives, artwork, and poetry by their peers. With a strong focus on achieving optimum physical and mental well-being, each chapter concludes with strategies for making healthy changes in a hectic lifestyle.

Keeping Peace: Conflict Resolution and Peaceful Societies Around the World edited by Graham Kemp and Douglas P. Fry (New York: Routledge, 2003). Drawing from varied social and cultural experiences, this collection of ethnographies explores the beneficial results of peaceful conflict resolution practices.

The Kid's Guide to Social Action: How to Solve the Social Problems You Choose—and Turn Creative Thinking into Positive Action by Barbara A. Lewis (Minneapolis: Free Spirit Publishing, 1995). This book offers ideas and resources to help kids design and implement creative projects to improve their lives, schools, communities, and anything else they choose to change. Includes "Kids in Action" success stories—examples of real kids making a real difference.

Learning the Skills of Peacemaking: A K–6 Activity Guide to Resolving Conflicts, Communicating, and Cooperating by Naomi Drew (Rolling Hills Estates, CA: Jalmar Press, 1995). A clear, detailed resource for counselors, parents, and educators that promotes open, effective communication for students in real-life situations through role-play activities, peer mediation exercises, and information on parent involvement and workshops.

The Nature of School Bullying: A Cross-National Perspective edited by P. K. Smith, Y. Morita, J. Junger-Tas, D. Olweus, R. Catalano, and P. Slee (New York: Routledge, 1998). Designed as a resource for educators, this book compiles bullying definitions and data from 19 countries. It specifically addresses the different types of school bullying, related statistics, and suggested intervention techniques.

The New Conflict Cookbook: A Parent/Teacher Guide for Helping Young People Deal with Anger and Conflict by Thomas Crum, Judith Warner, Cheryl Birmingham, and Christine Steerman (New York: Aiki Works, 2000). It's important to develop skills for dealing with disagreements at home, at school, and with friends. Based on an inclusive mind/body approach, the Magic of Conflict techniques encourage healthy expression of opinions with the understanding that disagreement and conflict, when handled respectfully, can help us grow.

The Peaceful Classroom in Action by Naomi Drew (Rolling Hills Estates, CA: Jalmar Press, 1999). This practical activity book helps teachers establish and maintain a peaceful, productive learning environment. With an emphasis on mutual respect and conflict resolution, this book helps students build oral and written communication skills.

Ready-to-Use Self-Esteem and Conflict Solving Activities for Grades 4–8 by Beth Teolis (Indianapolis, IN: Jossey-Bass, 2002). Specially designed for educators and counselors working with at-risk students, this book includes a step-by-step curriculum, goal setting activities, and strategies to improve self-esteem and promote peaceful solutions to conflict. Fun and effective with individuals, small groups, or the whole class.

A Teacher's Guide to Anger Management by Paul Blum (New York: Routledge, 2001). This book is specifically designed for classroom management and school-wide initiatives to end behavior problems. It encourages adolescents to develop healthy, emotionally expressive skills and outlines school pilot programs to cope with the cycle of anger.

What Do You Stand For? A Kid's Guide to Building Character by Barbara A. Lewis (Minneapolis: Free Spirit Publishing, 1997). Readers learn to build traits such as empathy, citizenship, leadership, and respect with an emphasis on self-discovery and volunteering.

Yoga Journal's Yoga Basics: The Essential Beginner's Guide to Yoga for a Lifetime of Health and Fitness by Mara Carrico and the *Yoga Journal* Editors (New York: Henry Holt & Company, 1997). A fundamental text with over 140 photographs, this easy-to-follow guide takes the reader from philosophy to poses, detailing the nine varieties of Hatha Yoga to improve physical and mental well-being.

Web sites

Do Something: Young People Changing the World
www.dosomething.org
Do Something works "to inspire young people to believe that change is possible." The organization has a national leadership training program and specially designed "challenges" for students in community building, health, and the environment. Educators and youth leaders can log on and access activities and curricula to complement each "challenge."

Free the Children
www.freethechildren.org
Originally founded by a 12-year-old boy looking to make a difference, Free the Children is an international organization committed to fighting child poverty and exploitation. Connect with people from around the world to learn how you can help children in need.

The Gay, Lesbian and Straight Education Network (GLSEN)

www.glsen.org

Devoted to GLBTQ youth, this organization has taken on a strategic plan to stamp out anti-GLBTQ bullying, name-calling, and harassment in American schools. Their site includes a student section with links to local organizations and a forum for interactive discussions. Educators will find a curriculum guide as well as links to additional resources.

The Giraffe Project

www.giraffe.org

The Giraffe Project works to inspire K–12 students to be courageous, active citizens. Their site includes helpful resources and extraordinary stories about heroes of all ages who are willing to stick out their necks to help others.

My Hero

www.myhero.com

This site introduces stories of remarkable people who've made a difference in the world, their communities, and the lives of others. Includes detailed lesson plans and activities to inspire students of all ages.

Youth Activism Project

www.youthactivism.com

This national clearinghouse site is full of information and advice for getting youth motivated and mobilized. Includes resources for kids, teens, parents, educators, and mentors.

WORKING OUT CONFLICTS SURVEY

Your age: _____   Are you a: (circle one)   boy   girl

Where you live: (circle one)   Urban Area   Suburb   Small Town   Rural Area

1. How often do you see kids having conflicts such as arguments or fights? (circle one)

Often	**Sometimes**	**Not very often**
(several times a day)	(at least once a day)	(less than once a day)

2. How often do YOU have conflicts such as arguments or fights? (circle one)

Often	**Sometimes**	**Not very often**
(several times a day)	(at least once a day)	(less than once a day)

3. Have you ever been picked on by other kids? What happened, and what did you do about it? (explain in as much detail as possible)_____

_____

_____

_____

4. How do you feel when kids have conflicts? (explain)_____

_____

_____

_____

5. Who do you usually see having conflicts? _____

_____

_____

_____

6. What do kids usually do when they have a conflict or trouble with someone?

_____

_____

_____

7. What do YOU usually do when you have a conflict with someone? _____

_____

_____

_____

more ⟶

8. Which best states how you feel? (please check any that apply)

❑ I think I work out problems with people pretty well.

❑ I wish I was better at working out problems with others.

❑ I'm not very good at working out problems with others.

❑ I'd like to learn more about working out problems with others.

9. What three things do you or your friends or siblings have the most conflicts about? _____

_____

_____

10. What, if anything, does your school do to help kids to solve problems or conflicts peacefully? For example, do they have a peer mediation program? _____

_____

_____

11. Do you think learning how to resolve conflicts peacefully is important? Why or why not? _____

_____

_____

12. What do you most want to learn about resolving conflicts? _____

_____

_____

13. On a scale of 1–10, how mean do you think kids generally are to each other? Please put an X on the scale below.

1	2	3	4	5	6	7	8	9	10

not mean at all   the meanest it's possible to be

14. How do you think we can get kids to stop being mean to each other? _____

_____

_____

_____

Index

A

Abdominal breathing. *See* deep breathing
Affirmations
  importance of, 47–48
  used in Day-by-Day Plan, 83–89
Anger
  fueling, 54
  results of, 55
  understanding, 53
Anger management, 53–55
  checklist (reproducible), 55
  importance of, 102, 107
  review sheet answers, 103, 105
  review sheet (reproducible), 97, 102
  skills sheet for improving (reproducible), 87
  See also "Stop, Breathe, Chill" technique
Apologizing, 47
Assertiveness, 26–28
Assessments
  of body language and facial expressions, 52
  of listening skills (reproducible), 35–36
  pre- and post-program, 24
Automatic writing exercises, 18, 32

B

Blame and I-messages, 41
Body language
  assessment of, 52
  moods and, 15
Brainstorming, 47–49
Breathing. *See* deep breathing
Bullying
  checklists (reproducible), 73
  responding to, 74–75
  review sheet answers, 104, 105
  review sheet (reproducible), 99, 102
  roles in, 70, 71–72
  school-wide projects to stop, 72, 77
  skills sheet for stopping (reproducible), 89
  standing up for person being bullied, 71–72
  understanding, 68–69, 102, 107
Bystanders, 70

C

Calming techniques
  Light Shield, 59
  Peaceful Place visualization, 63–65, 66, 67
  Peace Shield
    review sheet answers, 104
    review sheet (reproducible), 97
    understanding, 58–59
  practicing with visualizations, 28
  schedule for practicing, 67
  "Stop, Breathe, Chill" technique
    Dignity Stance and, 27
    review sheet answers, 103
    review sheet (reproducible), 97

    role play, 23
    understanding, 22–23
    visualization, 54, 57
Challenging students, 4–5
Compassion, expressing, 71–72, 75
Confidentiality, 3
Conflict resolution
  importance of learning, 11–12
  importance of teaching, ix
  progress assessment (reproducible), 24
  requirements for, 15
  review sheet answers, 103
  review sheet (reproducible), 93
  school-wide projects about, 72, 76–77
Conflicts
  incidence in schools of, ix
  observing, 14–15
  observing (reproducible), 13, 46
  record of (reproducible), 25
  review sheet answers, 104–105
  review sheet (reproducible), 101–102
  triggers of, 15, 17, 93, 103
Conflict solvers
  action plan for, 81–82
  interviewing, 29
  learning from, 31–32
  review sheet answers, 103, 104, 105
  review sheets (reproducible), 94, 99, 102
  role play, 23
Curriculum, coordinating with, 1–2

D

Day-by-Day Plan
  affirmations for, 83–89
  review sheet (reproducible), 100
  understanding, 81–82
Deep breathing
  importance of, 5
  practicing, 27
  "Stop, Breathe, Chill" technique
    Dignity Stance and, 27
    review sheet answers, 103
    review sheet (reproducible), 97
    role play, 23
    understanding, 22–23
    visualization, 54, 57
  during visualizations, 49, 64
Dignity Stance
  practicing, 28, 75
  review cards (reproducible), 30
  role play, 32
  understanding, 26–27
Discussion guidelines, 4

E

Empowerment statements
    importance of, 47–48
    used in Day-by-Day Plan, 83–89
Evaluations. *See* assessments
Exit lines, 32, 74–75

F

Facial expressions
    assessment of, 52
    moods and, 15
Federal education mandates, 1–2
5/25 secret, 66–67
Forgiveness, 47, 78–80

G

Ground rules
    for role plays, 3–4
    for sessions, 2–5
    for Win/Win Guidelines, 40, 41
Guardians, explaining program to, 5, 7–8

I

"I Heard You Say," 39
I-messages
    review sheet answers, 103, 105
    review sheet (reproducible), 96, 101
    using, 40–42, 44
Interviews
    with conflict solvers, 29
    "Staying Out of Fights," 59

L

Light Shield, 59
Listening skills
    assessing, 35–36, 37
    good, 101, 105
    reflective, 37–39
    review sheet for improving answers, 103, 105
    review sheet for improving (reproducible), 95, 101
    skills sheet for improving (reproducible), 85
    techniques, 34
    understanding, 33
    using, 34

M

Mandela, Nelson, 79
Mentors, 67, 77
Moods, 15

N

Nonverbal language
    assessment of, 52
    moods and, 15

P

Parents, explaining program to, 5, 7–8
Peaceful Place
    school-wide project, 77
    visualization, 63–65, 66, 67

Peace Shield
    review sheet answers, 104
    review sheet (reproducible), 97
    understanding, 58–59

R

Reactions
    vs. responses, 17, 22
Reflective listening
    review sheet answers, 105
    review sheet (reproducible), 101
    using, 37–39
Responsibility, taking
    review sheet (reproducible), 46, 52, 102
    understanding, 44–45, 47
Role plays
    about bullying, 71, 74, 75
    about conflict solvers, 23
    about teasing, 69
    of actual conflicts, 18
    applying Win/Win Guidelines, 50–51
    focusing on taking responsibility, 45
    ground rules for, 3–4
    observation sheets (reproducible), 52
    overcoming blocks to willingness, 20
    overview of, 3
    using Dignity Stance, 27, 32
    using exit lines, 32
    using reflective listening, 38
    using "Stop, Breathe, Chill," 23

S

Safety
    absence from school and, ix
    creating atmosphere of, during sessions, 2–3, 14
    school-wide projects about, 77
Sarcasm and I-messages, 41
School-wide projects
    about conflict resolution, 72, 76–77
    for creating atmosphere of safety, 77
    for mentor program, 77
    to stop bullying, 72, 77
    to stop teasing, 69, 77
    using Win/Win Guidelines, 77
Secret of 5/25, 66–67
Sessions
    adapting, 1, 3
    ground rules for, 2–5
    structure of, 2
"Staying Out of Fights" interview, 59
"Stop, Breathe, Chill" technique
    Dignity Stance and, 27
    review sheet answers, 103
    review sheet (reproducible), 97
    role play, 23
    understanding, 22–23
    visualization, 54, 57
Stress
    effects of (reproducible), 62
    understanding, 60–61

Stress management
    importance of, 102, 107
    review sheet answers, 104, 105
    review sheet (reproducible), 98, 102
    skills sheet (reproducible), 88
    using Peaceful Place visualization for, 63–65, 66, 67

T

Teasing
    dealing with, 68–69
    school-wide projects about, 69, 77
Title IV—21st Century Schools: "Safe and Drug-Free
        Schools and Communities," 1–2
Turnaround, sparking, 37–39, 40

V

Verbal aggression, responding to, 26–28
Violence in school and culture, ix
Visualizations
    Light Shield, 59
    Peaceful Place, 63–65, 66, 67
    Peace Shield, 58–59
    practicing, 28
    "Stop, Breathe, Chill," 54, 57

W

Walking away, 32
Willingness
    overcoming blocks to, 19–21, 93, 103
    understanding, 15, 17–18

Win/Win Guidelines

Win/Win Guidelines
    applying, 50–52
    brainstorming solutions with, 47–49
    brainstorming solutions with (reproducible), 49
    business cards, 51
    dialogs, 54
    introducing, 40–43
    review sheet answers, 103
    review sheet (reproducible), 96
    rules review cards (reproducible), 43
    school-wide projects using, 77
    skills sheet for practicing (reproducible), 86
    taking responsibility, 44–46, 47
Word Walls, 60, 61

Y

"Yes, But" questions, 51
You-messages, 41

Z

Zingers, 56–57
    review sheet answers, 103–104
    review sheet (reproducible), 97

About the Author

Naomi Drew, M.A., is a well-known expert on conflict resolution, peacemaking, and parenting. She is also the author of *Learning the Skills of Peacemaking* (Jalmar Press, 1995), *Peaceful Parents, Peaceful Kids* (Kensington, 2000), and *Hope and Healing: Peaceful Parenting in an Uncertain World* (Citadel, 2002). Naomi has been featured in magazines and newspapers and on radio and television. A former teacher, she served as a parenting expert for "Classroom Close-ups," an Emmy-winning public television show.

Naomi acts as a consultant to school districts, leads seminars, and runs parenting and anti-bullying workshops. She headed the New Jersey State Bar Foundation's Conflict Resolution Advisory panel for eight years and taught public school for twenty-four years. She has worked with thousands of kids, parents, teachers, and administrators across the country for over twenty years. Her e-newsletter, *Peaceful Parents,* has broad international readership.

Her Web site, *www.learningpeace.com,* is a popular resource for those who want to create peace in their homes and schools. She has two grown sons and lives in New Jersey.

Other Great Books from Free Spirit

The Kids' Guide to Working Out Conflicts
How to Keep Cool, Stay Safe, and Get Along
by Naomi Drew, M.A.
Proven ways to avoid conflict and defuse tough situations, written by an expert on conflict resolution and peacemaking. Includes tips and strategies for dealing with bullies, lessening stress, and more. For ages 10–14. *$13.95; 160 pp.; softcover; illus.; 7" x 9"*

The Bully Free Classroom
Over 100 Tips and Strategies for Teachers K–8
by Allan L. Beane, Ph.D.
Positive and practical, this solution-filled book can make any classroom a place where all students are free to learn without fear. It spells out 100 proven strategies teachers can start using immediately. Includes true stories, checklists, resources, and reproducible handout masters. For teachers, grades K–8. *$19.95; 176 pp.; softcover; 8½" x 11"*

CD-ROM
This CD-ROM includes all 34 of the reproducible forms from the book. Teachers can print them out when they need them and even customize forms for their classrooms and students. *$15.95; Macintosh and PC compatible, 5" CD-ROM, 34 reproducible handout masters.*

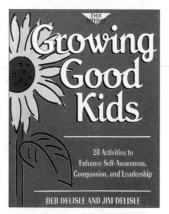

Growing Good Kids
28 Activities to Enhance Self-Awareness, Compassion, and Leadership
by Deb Delisle and Jim Delisle, Ph.D.
Created by teachers and classroom-tested, these fun and meaningful enrichment activities build children's skills in problem solving, decision making, cooperative learning, divergent thinking, and communication. For grades 3–8. *$21.95; 168 pp.; softcover; illus.; 8½" x 11"*

Stick Up for Yourself!
Every Kid's Guide to Personal Power and Positive Self-Esteem
Revised and Updated
by Gershen Kaufman, Ph.D., Lev Raphael, Ph.D., and Pamela Espeland
Simple text teaches assertiveness, responsibility, relationship skills, choice making, problem solving, and goal setting. For ages 8–12.
$11.95; 128 pp.; softcover; illus.; 6" x 9"

Teacher's Guide
A 10-Part Course in Self-Esteem and Assertiveness for Kids
Revised and Updated
by Gershen Kaufman, Ph.D., Lev Raphael, Ph.D., and Pamela Espeland
For teachers, grades 3–7.
$19.95; 128 pp.; softcover; 8½" x 11"